CHRISTIAN HOMES
ARE THE
VESTIBULES OF HEAVEN

M. F. McKNIGHT

Published By:

GOSPEL ADVOCATE COMPANY
Nashville, Tennessee 37202
1982

ACKNOWLEDGMENT

The author makes no claim for originality. It is my hope that teachers and preachers everywhere will teach such lessons to all of God's children.

I wish to gratefully acknowledge the unselfish work of Martha Pitts, Annette Fox, and Billie Mayes in preparation of these manuscripts.

I shall be eternally indebted to those who studied these subjects before me.

M. F. McKNIGHT

DEDICATION

This book is dedicated to my wife, two
daughters, and two sons. They truly
make my home a vestibule of heaven.

TABLE OF CONTENTS

WHAT IS MARRIAGE?
(Ephesians 5:22-31)

INTRODUCTION:
- A. We intend to define
- B. We need to understand
- C. We are not taught as we should be
  1. More important to be the right person than to find the right person
  2. The honeymoon and the 20th anniversary
  3. The Chinese philosophy

I.MARRIAGE IS THE APPLICATION OF THE GOLDEN RULE TO A VERY INTIMATE AND TENDER RELATIONSHIP:
- A. One word to guarantee a successful marriage
  1. "Ours"
  2. Let no one else share that which is yours alone
- B. Social preparation
- C. Spiritual preparation

II.A BIBLE DEFINITION OF MARRIAGE:
- A. Marriage is a covenant establishing a home
  1. Genesis 2:22
  2. Matthew 19:5-6
  3. Ephesians 5:31
- B. Marriage is more than a civil contract
  1. Matthew 19:6
  2. Romans 7:2

III.MARRIAGE IS THE PERMANENT UNION OF TWO PERSONALITIES UNDER GOD'S LAW AND BEFORE MEN:
- A. It is an opportunity for happiness

B. Marriage is the relationship between a man and woman
   1. Independence is equal
   2. Dependence is mutual
   3. Obligation is reciprocal

IV. THE ALL-INCLUSIVE DEFINITION:
A. Can be had by careful personal preparation, careful selection of a mate, and diligent effort
B. There are 1,200 divorces a day in America

CONCLUSION:
A. Church is the bride of Jesus
B. Hebrew wedding customs
C. Application to us
D. Tragedy of not being prepared for the great wedding feast

WHAT IS MARRIAGE?
(Ephesians 5:22-31)
INTRODUCTION

A. In the lesson this morning, we hope to answer the question, "What is marriage?" Some reasons that we are spending time in discussion of such things is because they are very fundamental, because they are found in the Word of God, and because they touch the lives of each and every one of us.

B. The home is a mighty institution, ordained of God for the happiness and for the well being of the human family. Yet, many homes as we find them today are not blessings to those who make up their membership, nor to the community, the nation, or the world. One marriage counselor, whom I suppose has done more in this particular field than anyone else in the United States, says that all marriages fall into one of four classifications. He says one out of every four marriages ends in divorce, one out of every four marriages ends in separation, one out of every four marriages has quarreling and bickering but they continue to live together, and one out of every four marriages is a success.

In other words, he suggests that your chances for having a home as God would have it are one in four. Your marriage and mine falls into one of these four classifications. It will either end in divorce, separation, or will exist in strained relations or it will be a home as God would have it. There are no other classifications. One other man, a Dr. Adams who is a teacher and professor of psychology at Penn State, makes this observation; that one out of six marriages is extremely happy. This certainly does not contradict what we have just noticed—one out of four is a happy marriage—but this man says one out of six is extremely happy.

C. As a boy I never heard a sermon on the home as God would have it. I never heard a lesson on marriage in the Sunday school classroom or from the pulpit. For that reason, we want to give to you suggestions of God in regard to preparing for marriage if you have not yet taken this step.

I know that many times we feel we can go out into life and will find the right person and our marriage will be a success. Young people, may I suggest this to you. There is something far more important to the happiness of your marriage than *finding* the right person and that is *being* the right person. We feel that if we can just find him or her that it will be all right, but if you will just *be* the one you ought to be it will be all right. I don't know what kind of success you are going to have in finding that one, but I know you can make the personal and the social and the spiritual preparation which will insure a happy home, if you will exercise some care in selecting a mate. Many young people go about the selection of a mate with the romantic and egocentric attitude of getting rather than giving. Those who have the "gimme" attitude haven't grown up emotionally enough for marriage; I don't care if you are 16 or 66. You just haven't grown up enough for marriage. Marriage is an institution for adults and not for children. Many people need to divorce themselves first of all and then they will know how to live with others much better. Many times self is the biggest problem or obstacle to a successful marriage. When we are contemplating marriage our eyes are fixed upon the honeymoon and very few eyes are fixed upon the 20th wedding anniversary. I know that instead of being so absorbed with the honeymoon we would fix our eyes upon the 20th anniversary then it would rob marriage of some of its glory, glitter, and glamour, but it would appear to us in a very realistic form. You make a lot of plans and preparations for that honeymoon; what kind of plans and preparations do you make for the 20th anniversary?

A Chinese statesman, Li Hung Ching, was talking about the parent arranged marriages in China where there is practically no divorce. He said the marriages in China begin like this. "It is like putting a kettle of cold water on a hot stove, and it begins to warm up and boil and it continues to remain hot. But marriages in America are like putting a kettle of boiling water on a cold stove, and it begins to cool off and it isn't long until it is cold." Think about that. Sometimes we go at it with the wrong attitude. "I think that marriage is the golden rule, applied to a very intimate relationship." This is our first definition of marriage. I am going to give you a lot of partial definitions and then in a few minutes I will give you one which I hope is conclusive, and includes all of these others.

I.

A. Marriage is the application of the golden rule to a very intimate relationship. If I were to ask you what one word in your vocabulary will guarantee the success of a happy home more than any other word, what would you tell me? I am talking about a word now. What word in your vocabulary, husbands and wives, brides and grooms, boyfriends and girlfriends, what one word in your vocabulary will insure the success of your home more than any other one word? Many of you would say, "love". Love is an important word, but the act of love is far less important than the word that I am talking about. There is one word that love will cause us to speak. This one word which will contribute to our success and happiness is OURS—O U R S. *Our* income, *our* home, *our* family, *our* house, *our* car, *our* vacation, *our* friends, *our* religion, *our* Sunday school class. There is no other one word which you need to develop and to use more than that one in making the home a success. I plead with you, husbands and wives, preserve the sacredness of your own home, of your own hearts, of your own married state with all diligence. Let no one, not even father, or mother, sister or brother, presume to come between you. Let no one share the joys and the sorrows that belong to you two and to you two alone . . . . OURS . . . . . if you please.

B. In regard to the social preparation for marriage, I suggest you choose your associates carefully. I know what you think, young people. You think that someday I am going to find that perfect one and I will marry him or her. The chances are you are going to marry someone no better than yourself and then look what a mess you are going to be in. Chances are they are going to be human, and they are going to have shortcomings and frailties and weaknesses, and many a young lady has been disappointed. It happens the other way some, but more often this way. Many a young lady has taken some old boy who isn't worth much and she has decided that she will marry him and then she will reform him. She then finds out that it is impossible to make a good house out of shabby, sorry, rotten, cheap, inferior material. You just can't do it. No contractor is good enough to take rotten material and make a beautiful building out of it.

C. In regard to the spiritual preparation, we say "Be a Christian." Someone has said that marriages are made in heaven, but I want you to know that the maintenance work is carried on by man and it takes effort on the part of all of us. Marriage is the greatest of all human contracts. If it had no spiritual significance, if it had no eternal significance whatsoever, marriage would still be the greatest of all human contracts. There is no other contract which affects the lives of so many and the destiny and the happiness of so many. It is the greatest of all human contracts. Number One, because it originated in the mind of God. Number two, because our national welfare depends upon it, society depends upon it. Listen to the old pagan philosopher, Cicero; he says that "the very first bond of society is matrimony". If pagans could understand this, it looks like God's children could. In ancient Rome during the decaying days, bachelors had to be fined in order to make them marry. A very high tax was placed upon bachelorhood because the pagan Romans could see their government and their society falling apart at the seams. Socrates said, "By all means, marry. If you get a good wife, you will become very happy; if you get a bad one, you will become a philosopher; both of which are good for a man." I taught a series to a high school class on the home as God would have it. One boy went home and said, "Mother, I just learned one thing in Brother McKnight's class." "What is that?" He said, "Don't ever get married." I am not attempting to discourage marriage, but I am trying to get you to give it the same consideration that you give any ordinary business deal. Certainly it deserves that. None of us would invest $1,000 in some business without first studying about it for a little while and wondering, "Is it safe?" "Will this business last?" "What about my partner, is he dependable?" But we jump into marriage some times without even that much consideration, and it is the greatest of all human contracts because it lasts a lifetime. It is the greatest of all human contracts because it has eternal consequences. The influences which you set in motion when you say "I do" at the altar will last throughout eternity.

II.

A. For a Bible definition of marriage, I began to search the scriptures. What is a scriptural definition for it? The Bible tells us that marriage is a covenant establishing a home. This is as simple as I can make it. It is a contract between a man and a woman establishing a home. We find in Genesis the second chapter and beginning in about verse 22, God has taken a rib from Adam's side and from it He has fashioned woman, and God has awakened Adam, and Adam looks upon his wife for the first time. Genesis 2:23, "Behold, this is bone of my bone and flesh of my flesh, and henceforth she shall be called woman because she was taken out of man. (Now the definition) For this cause (the cause of marriage, the cause of establishing a human home upon this earth) shall a man leave his father and his mother and shall cleave to his wife and they shall be one flesh." This is the best Bible definition for marriage that I can find. I realize it is repeated and a little bit added to it by Jesus Christ in Matthew 19:5-6. Jesus said, "For this cause (that of marriage) shall a man leave his father and his mother and shall cleave to his wife and they twain shall be one flesh. Wherefore, they are no more twain, but one flesh. What, therefore, God has joined together let no man put asunder." Then in Ephesians 5:31, "For this cause (that is marriage) shall a man leave his father and his mother, shall cleave to his wife and they two shall be one flesh." There is the scriptural definition. God has written a lot about marriage and about the various aspects of it, which we intend to cover in lessons to come.

B. Marriage is more than just a civil contract. Marriage is more than just an agreement between a man and a woman to live together as husband and wife. God has written some requirements. He has given some restrictions. We just read one of them, Matthew 19:6, "What therefore God hath joined together let no man put asunder." Romans 7:2, "A woman is bound by the law to her husband as long as they both shall live, but if the husband be dead, she is freed from the law of her husband." Is marriage an institution of the church or of the state? The answer is, of course, neither. Marriages were made before there was a church or before there was a state. Marriages are made in heaven, God has given the laws, the rules and the regulations governing it for our good. He knew what we needed; He knows what is best for us.

III.

A. Now, let's notice some other definitions for marriage. What is marriage? Marriage is the permanent union of two personalities under God's law and before man. A permanent union of two personalities under God's law and before man . . . two minds with but a single thought . . . two hearts that beat as one . . . OURS, if you please. It calls for a lot of faith, a lot of love, a lot of forbearance and constant cooperation. It will never drift along and get any better. It takes work, diligent effort on the part of all. Marriage is an opportunity for happiness, not a gift. Marriage is where a man and a woman unite their forces together in the mutual pursuit of happiness. Just because you get married doesn't guarantee that you will be happy. Marriage is an indissoluble union between a man and a woman.

B. Someone has defined marriage like this: Marriage is the relationship between a man and a woman in which independence is equal, dependence is mutual and obligation is reciprocal. "There is neither bond, nor free, Jew nor Greek, male nor female ..." We all stand independent of everyone else in our relationship to God, even husband or wife cannot make us go to heaven or make us go to hell. Independence here is equal, dependence is mutual and we will be talking about what wives can depend upon husbands for and what husbands can depend upon wives for; obligation is reciprocal. I have a right to expect certain things of my wife; she has a right to expect certain things of me and one of these, just one among many, is found in I Corinthians 7:1-5.

IV.

A. Now hear this definition. I hope it is all inclusive. What is marriage? "Marriage is an agreement by which a man and woman consent to live together as husband and wife for the purpose of establishing a home, mutually accepting all the responsibility which the relationship involves, and properly expecting all the rights and privileges incident thereto." I am sorry that it had to be so complicated. This is the most inclusive definition which I know. I want to name three things which will guarantee your marriage to be a success. First of all, a careful personal preparation, divorce yourself if you have to, and you will have to. Secondly, a very careful selection of a mate. Then diligent effort on the part of both. No business can succeed without diligent effort. It is a rare, rare thing, I would say, if a business succeeds without someone putting forth some diligent effort to see it through. It is a rare, rare thing for a marriage to succeed unless someone puts forth diligent effort to see it through. So, first of all, very careful preparation, careful selection and then diligent effort on the part of both.

B. Because people have failed in these, the divorce courts are grinding the American home into oblivion at the rate of 1200 a day. Twelve hundred times a day a judge's gavel pounds the bench and the sentence is pronounced, "Divorce granted" and another home is torn up.

CONCLUSION

A. Now, the lesson is yours but I want you to think about this before we extend the invitation. In the reading a while ago, Paul said that this is a great mystery, the relationship of husband and wife, but he said, "I speak concerning Christ and the church." All the way through the Bible we find God's relationship to His people being likened unto marriage. We find it mentioned in numerous places, Isaiah 54:1, Isaiah 62:5, Jeremiah 2:32, John 3:29, Ephesians 5:30-31 and in many other places. God refers to the relationship between Him and His people as being marriage. I want you to know that from the very foundation of the world, that Jesus Christ had accepted His people to be His bride . . . . the church to be His holy bride. The wedding was announced over and over again in the Old Testament and the dowry was paid on Calvary. Jesus purchased the church with His own blood. He is coming again some day to claim His bride and the church is to prepare herself; Revelation 19, "The church stood before the Lord prepared as a bride adorned for her husband, pure and clean, righteous, clothed in white robes which is the righteousness of the saints," John the revelator said.

B. The Hebrew marriage went like this. Here is a man and a woman who come together and they become espoused which is more binding than our engagement. They exchange the vows of marriage, but we just call them engaged, because then the groom goes back to his home and the bride stays at hers. There is an interval before the marriage supper is to take place. They are considered husband and wife. They are espoused. Then, if the groom has not done so, he pays the dowry to her parents. On the night for the wedding feast, he and his fellows come through the streets of the city in the wedding party carrying torches and singing. They come to her house and take the bride to his house and there they have the marriage supper or the wedding feast and the celebration often lasts seven days, and on some occasions 14 days.

C. Now, here is where we are in that relationship with God. The announcement of the wedding has already taken place. We have become espoused to Christ, II Corinthians 11:2, Paul said, "I am jealous over you with a godly jealousy for I have espoused you unto one husband, Jesus Christ." We are in the interval of waiting for this marriage feast and when He comes again all those who have been called, all those who have been bidden, shall come to that feast. Jesus is going to come for this marriage feast with His fellows, with a teeming host of the angels of heaven and He is going to call the church, His pure and chaste virgin, for His bride. There is going to be a wedding feast and celebration that will last, not for 7 days or 14 days, but throughout eternity. Only those who are ready will enter in.

D. You remember the story Jesus told in Matthew 24 about the torch bearers at the wedding. They came, five of them wise and five of them foolish, and the bridegroom tarried. He has been tarrying now for 1900 years, how much longer He will tarry I do not know, but I know He is coming again. All the torch bearers slumbered and slept and about midnight a great cry was made, "Behold, the bridegroom cometh," and they awakened and they rubbed the sleep out of their eyes and they began to trim their lamps. The foolish ones found that their lamps had sputtered and gone out because they had not made adequate preparation. The wise ones had oil and the foolish ones wanted some of their oil. They answered, "No, we may not have enough to go around. You go into the city and there you buy from those that have to sell, provide your own." No one can provide your works of righteousness for you. You will have to do that yourself. The five foolish ones went into the city to buy oil and while they were gone the bridegroom came. Notice the next verse: "And those that were ready went in with him to the feast." Those who were thinking about beginning to get ready had the door closed in their faces.

Are you ready for this marriage feast? Some day He is going to come again and those who are ready will go with Him into the feast and it will be a very happy and joyous occasion, but those who are thinking about getting ready will be left out.

STUDY QUESTIONS
WHAT IS MARRIAGE?

1. Give the best reason you know for studying things concerning the marital relationship.
2. Do you feel this subject is studied enough?
3. What percent of marriages are termed a success?
4. Which do you consider the more important, finding the right person to marry, or being the right person?
5. Who is usually the greatest obstacle to a successful marriage?
6. What one word will contribute more to our marital happiness than any other?
7. Why is marriage the most important of all human contracts?
8. What is the Bible definition of marriage?
9. How would you define marriage?
10. Tell of the Hebrew marriage customs.

***

The great essentials of happiness are something to do, something to love, and something to hope for.

THE PURPOSE OF MARRIAGE
(Genesis 2:18-24)

INTRODUCTION:
- A. Fundamental purpose
- B. Other purposes

I. COMPANIONSHIP:
- A. Genesis 2:18
    1. "Woman" means "of man"
    2. Natural to desire a mate
- B. Proverbs 18:22
    1. Index to a happy home
    2. Cure ills in home and cure all ills

II. SATISFACTION OF NATURAL DESIRES:
- A. Proverbs 5:19 and I Corinthians 7:2-5
    1. Husband and wife find satisfaction in each other
    2. Birth control
- B. Hebrews 13:4

III. GENESIS 1:28 "BE FRUITFUL, AND MULTIPLY, AND REPLENISH THE EARTH . . . ."
- A. A continuous admonition (Jeremiah 29:6)
- B. Truth must be instilled in children by parents (Genesis 18:19)
- C. Many parents wait until it is too late
    1. Deuteronomy 4:9
    2. Ephesians 6:1
    3. I Peter 2:13
    4. Hebrews 5:8-9
    5. I Corinthians 3:16-17
- D. Teach them the story of salvation
- E. Provide a wholesome social atmosphere
    1. Do not just be negative
    2. Provide wholesome entertainment and guidance
    3. Children will marry from among their associates

SUMMARY:
CONCLUSION:
   A. Define a Christian home
   B. Are you interested more in material or spiritual welfare?

THE PURPOSE OF MARRIAGE
(Genesis 2:18—24)

A. The subject this morning is "Purpose Of Marriage". Actually, I suppose I should make that plural and say, "The Purposes Of Marriage". I think that everyone knows and understands that the fundamental purpose of marriage is the procreation of the human race; that is, the having of children.

B. But there are other purposes mentioned in God's Word subsidiary to this one and we want to talk about them this morning. I warn you in the beginning that there are some passages of scripture that I will not quote, I will elude to them in a general way and give you the passage and you may jot them down and read them in the privacy of your own home at your own convenience. Due to the nature of some of them, I feel it best just to tell you in a general way what is contained therein and you may want to make some notes about the scripture references as we go along.

I.

A. First of all, in our scripture reading this morning we noticed in Genesis 2:18 that there was "not found a help fit for Adam." The King James Version, of course, says "a helpmeet for Adam." The word "meet" in 1611 meant "fit". All of the animals in the kingdom had come by and Adam had named them, but there was not found a mate or a help fit for Adam. God said, "It is not good for man to live alone;" therefore, He caused a deep sleep to come upon Adam and He took from his side a rib and from it He fashioned woman and He closed the flesh thereof. Then He awakened Adam from his anesthesia and Adam looked upon the woman and said, "Behold, she is flesh of my flesh and bone of my bone. Henceforth, she shall be called woman because she was taken out of man." The word "woman" means "of man". We find here that God has decided that man needed a companion. We all can understand this. Anyone who withdraws from society is perverted, at least socially and perhaps morally. We know that it is natural in the very nature of things for man to desire a mate. When men, women, boys and girls begin to reach the age of maturity they have this desire implanted of God within them. We find them desiring someone to share life's fortunes and life's failures. Men are gregarious creatures. We like to be around other people, we like to do things with others. Of course, in the various stages of life our appetites for companionship change; but as we begin to reach maturity, it is then we find that man desires a mate. God through His very wonderful and very mysterious arrangement of the male and the female has provided for all the desires of love, companionship and fellowship one with the other. Through marriage, God expects the husband and the wife to find peace, pleasure and contentment in one another. God has so arranged it that all of these desires of the flesh can be fulfilled legitimately, scripturally and morally in this relationship.

B. We read in Proverbs 18:22, "Whoso findeth a wife, findeth a good thing." In the next chapter, Proverbs 19:14, "A prudent wife is from the Lord." These things are but an index to a happy home, and happy homes are but indexes to happy communities or society. There is not one ill in our society that cannot be traced to the home as the origin of it. Every ill that we have in society we find in the home. If we clean the homes up, we would be cleaning up society because society is made up of the homes.

II.

A. I believe the Bible teaches very emphatically that marriage is to provide for the natural appetites of the flesh. It is to provide satisfaction and gratification of the natural appetites of the flesh. Solomon said so very plainly in Proverbs 5:19 that one function of marriage was to provide for these appetites of the flesh. Then in I Corinthians 7:2-5, we find Paul very plainly saying that "in order that there be no fornication among you, let every man have his own wife and every wife her own husband." He continues by saying that they are to render due benevolence to each other and the wife hath not the power over her own body, but the husband; so likewise it is with the husband. He hath not the power over his own body, but the wife. If you notice and study just a little bit on verse 2 of I Corinthians 7, you will find the Bible teaching on birth control here. Many teach that it is wrong for a husband and wife to live together in the marital relationship except for the purpose of having children. But you notice that the Bible has mentioned a secondary reason for marriage. "In order that you might live chaste, pure, clean lives. As husbands and wives, let every man have his own wife and every wife her own husband. Defraud ye not one another," he says in verse 5, "unless it be with mutual consent that you might give yourselves to fasting and to prayer." Then he said, "Come together again as soon as feasible, lest Satan should tempt you in your incontinency." So, we can see that the Bible has very plainly taught that at least there are two purposes of marriage. One, companionship and another, the fulfillment of the gratifications of the natural appetites and passions of the flesh. Passion is not a dirty word. Passion means the normal appetites of the flesh. It means the God given desires of the flesh. The only time that it becomes dirty and cheap, vile and vulgar is when it is satisfied and gratified in some way that is ungodly, unscriptural, unholy, unlawful or immoral.

B. In Hebrews 13:4, "Let marriage be had in honor and the bed is not defiled." There is nothing at all wrong with the gratification of these natural desires of the flesh as long as it is within the lawful bonds of matrimony itself. Not only that, but there is another reason which we just mentioned and that is the procreation of the human race.

III.

A. God said, first of all, "Adam, you need a help fit for you. You need a companion, and in this companion you are to find gratification of these appetites of the flesh. And be fruitful and multiply and replenish the earth's population," Genesis 1:28. He continued that admonition to the children of Israel even throughout the Old Testament. In Jeremiah 29:6, we find it saying here,

"Take ye wives and beget sons and daughters and take ye wives for your sons and give your daughters to husbands that they may have sons and daughters." Why? "In order that ye may not diminish, but that ye may be increased upon the earth." So, marriage is for the purpose of reproduction. There is far more to it than **this**, but that is the basic purpose of it. Be fruitful, multiply, replenish the earth. Let your family name not become extinct, if at all possible. You know, there is something more important than just having children, though.

B. Basic, fundamental truths of life must be instilled by the parents into their children. God said of Abraham in Genesis 18:19 that "I know him, that he will command his household after him, that his children will have respect for him." God said that about Abraham, could He say that about you? "I know him, that he will command his household." He will be the head of the household; he is going to lead it in the way it should go; he is going to teach his children the things which they should know. This is very important. We must begin early in life in the training of the children who come our way.

One woman went to see one of our foremost educators after he had given a lecture, and she said, "Sir, I have a boy at home. He is 5 years old. When do you think I should begin to train him?"

And this educator said, "Hurry home, you have already wasted the best five years of his life."

C. Many people want to wait until their children are grown before they teach them. Many want to wait until the child is big enough to understand them. How sweet it is when a little child learns as some of his first words, "God", "Christ", "Bible", "church", and he learns to pray. These things should begin in the home. God so arranged it that we have our children more than anyone else. From the time your child and mine is born until he graduates from high school, he is awake 105,000 hours. During these 105,000 hours, do you know how many are spent under the direct influence and supervision of the home? 93,000.

He spends nearly 10,000 hours in school from the time he starts in the first grade until he graduates from high school. If you send him or take him to Sunday school every week, he will spend about 2,100 hours in Sunday school. I said that in order to say this. Parents, if we lose our children, let's not blame the public school teachers. We have our children 9 times as much under the direct influence and supervision of the home as do the school teachers. If we lose them, let's not blame the Sunday school teachers because we have them 45 times as much as the Sunday school teacher does during the waking hours of their lives.

God has taught us to teach our children. He has always demanded it even when they are quite little. Not only are parents to teach their children, but grandparents are to teach their grandchildren—He demanded it through the law of Moses and still does today (Deuteronomy 4:9). Paul said to Timothy, "When I think about the faith that you have, Timothy, I remember that it was first in your grandmother and then in your mother and now it dwells in you. That from a youth up both your grandmother and your mother have instructed you in the holy scriptures of God." Children must be taught parental obedience. This is a fundamental truth. Ephesians 6:1, "Children, obey your parents in the Lord for this is right." Children must first learn obedience in the home. It is according to God's divine arrangement of things that they should learn this. Children who do not learn parental obedience are the ones then who have trouble learning civil obedience. If they can be disobedient with parents and get away with it, they think they can be disobedient to civil law.

The juvenile delinquents are the ones who never learned obedience in the home. They think since they have gotten away with rebellion to authority as far as the home is concerned that they can get away with rebellion to authority in the civil government. God has demanded that children obey the parents and He has commanded also that children, and adults, obey the law or the civil statutes of the land. I Peter 2:13, ". . . be subject unto every ordinance of man." We could put a period there, it is pretty plain. I don't think any of us could misunderstand it. God said through the inspired pen of the apostle Peter, "Be subject unto every ordinance of man." Then He adds this phrase, ". . . for the Lord's sake." Don't you let someone point their finger at you and say, "You claim to be a Christian citizen and you hold in contempt the laws of man and the laws of God." Did you know that a person cannot obey God until they have first learned to obey the laws of the land? Obedience is not an easy lesson to learn. All of us have had to learn it. Jesus Christ Himself "learned obedience through the things which he suffered." (Hebrews 5:8 and 9) I know that some times we say that we love our children too much to teach them obedience, but we are just deceiving ourselves. If we love them, we will teach them obedience. We will train them in that way. We will teach them not only to be obedient to parents, but we will teach them also to be obedient to the laws of the land. It is pretty difficult to teach them, fathers and mothers, unless you are yourself obedient to these laws.

A man and his eleven year old son carried me to the airport in Nashville, Tennessee. I said, to the eleven year old boy, "Rusty, do you know what I like about you more than anything else?"

He said, "No, sir."

I said, "It is just that. Everyone I have heard you talk to since I have been in your home, you have said, 'Yes, sir', 'No, sir', 'Yes, ma'am', and 'No, ma'am.'" It is kind of unusual to find an eleven year old boy who is trained like that; who shows that much respect for his elders regardless of who they are and whether he knows them or not. Everybody he answered on every occasion was either, "Yes, sir", "Yes, ma'am", "No, ma'am". It makes an impression upon people. The God of Heaven intended that the younger people should have respect for older people. When we get to the lesson on GOD'S PLAN FOR THE AGED, we will talk about that particular thing. Just remember, the God of Heaven wants children to learn obedience in the home, to learn obedience to the civil statutes and then and then only can they learn divine obedience. That should be the ultimate aim. Any child who comes into our family, we should want to lead to eternal salvation. They just can't go to heaven until they first learn to obey their parents. You can't go to heaven until you first learn to obey your parents because you are disobeying God anytime that you disobey parents. You are disobeying God anytime that you disobey the statutes of the land in which we live.

A basic fundamental truth which parents ought to teach their children is that their bodies are the temples of the living God. In I Corinthians 3:16, "Know ye not that your body is the temple of God that the spirit of God dwells in you and if any man destroy the temple of God, him will God destroy."

Children should be taught proper habits to take care of their physical health. It is a sin to live in dissipation. It is a sin not to look after our health. Somebody says, "Well, now, what about overeating?" Anything that is detrimental to the health is sin. Our bodies are the temples of God. The Spirit of God dwells in us, if we are His children. This is the temple of God and if I destroy it, if I besmirch it with sin, God will destroy me. It is just that plain. Children ought to be taught proper eating habits and proper sleeping habits and proper habits of self–control. These are things which they have to learn at home. I know many parents who say, "Boy, I will be glad when this child of mine starts to school and maybe they can straighten him out." God pity the public school teachers who receive children such as that. The home is where God intended for them to learn obedience.

D. Another, basic fundamental thing which should be learned in the home is the story of salvation. Many parents are too busy with television, too busy with bridge clubs, too busy with study clubs, too busy with everything in this life to teach their children about God, to teach their children about the love of God, to teach their children what sin is. Today we live in an age in which sin is soft pedalled. "Everybody does it anyway and we don't want to call it sin because that is kind of a nasty word and we would rather just call it a mistake." Many parents even teach their children to sin and I will prove it to you when I preach on the children in the home. Children learn to lie from people who claim to be Christian parents. Children learn to cheat from people who claim to be Christian parents. Children learn to steal from people who claim to be Christian parents, and I will give you some cut and dried illustrations of it from people who are living and have done that very thing. We should teach our children about faith in Jesus Christ, repentance that will turn us toward Jesus Christ, confessing the name of Jesus Christ, being baptized into the name of Jesus Christ. We have so many people who will teach faith, repentance, confession and baptism and never mention Christ because Christ isn't the center and the heart of their life. That is just about as useless and futile as anything which I can think of. Teach somebody that they must believe—believe what? Believe in whom? Repent, turn toward whom? Confess. Confess what? Be baptized into what? Water? No, into the name of Jesus Christ. Make Christ the center and the heart of your life in your relationship with your family and teach them.

E. Another thing which parents forget, this is fundamental to our responsibility to our children and God, is to provide a wholesome social arrangement for our children in our homes. To many parents, discipline consists of this: "Now don't you do that, this or the other." What do you provide for your children to do? What do you provide for the young people to do? It will cost a little bit of time and money to provide something. Yes, it will. But I am thankful to God that there are people in Abilene, Texas, who on graduation night will provide a party, a good, clean, wholesome entertaining party for the juniors and seniors of the schools here in this city. I am grateful that there are men and women (some parents aren't interested enough) in this city interested enough in our children, our juniors and seniors to provide for them so that they won't feel so left out of the all—night revelry that goes on with the rest of the high school seniors. What do you do toward providing a wholesome social arrangement for your children? Anything? Do you just say, "Don't do this and don't do that?" You need something positive. You know Abraham and his wife were concerned about whom their boy would marry. They said to their servant, "We don't want Isaac to marry among the heathen. Go back to Haran and there get a wife for him from among our own people." They were concerned enough that they sent a servant nearly 400 miles round—trip to provide the right kind of a wife for their boy, Isaac. Christian parents ought to be concerned with just who the young people will marry. They are going to marry among the ones they associate with. What kind of associations do you provide for them? They,will date those whom they associate with and they will marry those they date. They are going to marry among those whom they associate with. Are you providing a wholesome environment for your boys and girls? Then don't wait until they begin to marry outside of Christ and then come to the preacher and ask him to go and talk to them and try to straighten up in about an hour's time what you have been 18 years in messing—up. God has given you this responsibility. I will do what I can as a preacher, but I will tell you right now you parents have far more influence than the preacher does. I am not saying this to add to the hurt that is in the heart of any of you who have lost your children. God forbid, but there are those of us who have our children now in the tender, formative years of their lives. Let us measure up to the responsibilities which God has given us now. We cannot violate the laws of God without paying for it. The fires of hell are kindled this side of the grave. There are those who have aches in their hearts that no amount of living can ever erase.

SUMMARY
So we have noticed in regard to marriage; first of all it is for companionship. Next, that the natural appetites of the flesh might be satisfied and gratified in each other. Next, that we are to produce children and that we are to teach them basic, fundamental truths concerning life. If you love your child, you will.

CONCLUSION
A. The best kind of environment which they can have is a Christian home. We have already defined a Christian home

as a place of unity—a Christian mother and father who are looking after the interest of the children. Whose wills and whose hearts are one and their sole purpose in life is to provide for their children spiritually and physically.

B. Recently I asked an elder about the welfare of one of his sons. He said, "My son is just doing fine. He is just making all kinds of money." I felt a bit nauseated. I wasn't interested in how much money he was making. I was interested in whether he was faithful to his God or not. I was interested in whether he had a Christian wife and was rearing his children in a Christian faith or not. How much money he made or how little, I cared not for, save just for the sake of interest. Too many parents today think when they provide a house, pay the grocery bill, pay the doctor bill, provide a motor scooter in junior high, a car in high school, and a new car in college, that they have really been a parent like they ought to have been. I want to say to you that a father who provides only materially for his family is a very poor excuse for a father indeed. Does your child have a Christian father? Does your child have a Christian mother? Are you providing the kind of environment you should? Are you fulfilling the God—given purpose for marriage in your life? If you are not, right now is a good time for you to start by rendering obedience to the gospel, by rededicating your life, by pledging yourself to the service of the Master, by confessing your sins and asking for the prayers of faithful brethren in your behalf. Whatever is lacking in your life, why don't you make it right, right now.

A house is built of logs and stone,
Of tiles and posts and piers,
A home is built of loving deeds,
That stand a thousand years.

Victor Hugo

STUDY QUESTIONS
THE PURPOSE OF MARRIAGE

1. What was the purpose of the creation of Eve?
2. What is the Bible position of birth control?
3. How many purposes for marriage can you think of?
4. Does having children fulfill our God-given responsibilities in marriage?
5. What supreme compliment did God pay Abraham's household? Can He say the same thing in regard to your home?
6. When is the best time to start training children about how to live?
7. Do grandparents have this responsibility to their grandchildren?
8. Which two women taught Timothy the Holy Scriptures?
9. Why should children obey their parents?
10. Do you believe parents should provide wholesome recreation and entertainment for their children? Do you?

MARRIAGE TO NON–CHRISTIANS

Brother Jess Hall recently carried some interesting figures in his (Dearborn Valley, Mich.) church bulletin. The following are taken from a survey by Alvin Jennings. In a check of 49 members of the church who married non–Christians the following are the results:

49 Christians married non–Christians
28 of these became unfaithful and left the Lord
21 of these remained faithful
9 of these were able to convert their spouses to the Lord

Think about this! 28 were lost to the Lord and only 9 converted the mate. Isn't this quite a gamble? No professional gambler would bet on such odds.

Published in Lubbock Morning Avalanche, March 14, 1956.-

LOVE ALONE CAN'T SOLVE ALL PROBLEMS
According to a survey of ministers and marriage counselors in Lubbock, your marriage will have the best chance for success if you:

1. Don't marry in a hurry. Take time to get to know each other well under all kinds of circumstances, not just on dates.
2. Solve your differences BEFORE marriage, not AFTER. Premarital discussions with a minister or a marriage counselor frequently can help you see danger spots which could wreck the marriage if not settled beforehand.
3. Avoid the non-realistic Hollywood romantic attitude that "if you're meant for each other and you're in love" everything else is bound to work out. Realize the only kind of lasting love in a marriage is Christian love, which involves honor, truth, forgiveness and respect toward your partner.

4. Grow up emotionally before you marry, not afterwards. Be mature enough to accept all the responsibility that goes with being married.
5. Cultivate the "our" attitude, rather than the "my" outlook. Selfishness destroys marriage. Be prepared to share literally everything with your partner.
6. Develop unity in your own home by doing things together and being genuinely interested in each other. Cultivate friends and recreation that you both enjoy. Be loyal to each other above everything else, even parents. Learn to disagree without being disagreeable.
7. Take a sober view of your finances before marriage. Try to devise a budget that suits you both. Don't live beyond your income and don't expect continued financial support from your parents.
8. Try to find a common religious faith. Then actively practice it together after marriage.
9. Make sure your understanding of sex doesn't include "misinformation". See a physican for a discussion on this topic.
10. Remember that marriage is a growing thing: You will either grow more in love with your partner each year or you will grow farther away from each other.

**

"If there is hope for the future of America; if there is to be peace and happiness in our homes, then we, as a nation, must turn to God and the practice of daily family prayer."

J. Edgar Hoover

PREPARATION FOR MARRIAGE

INTRODUCTION: LET US DEFINE MARRIAGE

A. God's definition
B. Civil definition
C. It is a contract
    1. More than one kind
    2. Conditions
    3. Originated with God
    4. Most important

I. IMPORTANCE OF PREPARATION:

A. Nothing can succeed without adequate preparation
B. Too little thought given to marriage preparation
C. Love alone cannot solve all the problems
D. Training grounds

II. WHAT TO DO IN PREPARATION:

A. Physical preparation
    1. Present a healthy body
    2. Wilfully injuring health is a sin
B. Mental preparation
    1. Marriage is for adults
    2. Develop character
    3. Keep morally pure
C. Social preparation
    1. Marriage is a social institution
    2. Do not date those you would not marry
D. Spiritual preparation: Be a Christian

III. DANGERS OF MARRYING A NON-CHRISTIAN:

A. No ideal home can be divided religiously
B. You will incur God's displeasure

IV. LET NO MAN PUT ASUNDER:
A. Matthew 19:6
B. Man is not to legislate in God's realm
C. Marriage is a permanent union
D. Consequences of civil court's rulings
   1. Nearly 400,000 broken homes yearly in U. S.
   2. Nearly 1,000,000 children rendered homeless yearly by divorce

CONCLUSION:
A. We have defined marriage and the need for preparation
B. We must prepare physically, mentally, morally, and spiritually
C. When we reject God's commands we always bring sorrow
D. You cannot break a home without breaking a heart

PREPARATION FOR MARRIAGE
INTRODUCTION

A. Marriage is a very difficult word to define. I searched through God's Word for a definition. The best is found in Genesis 2:24. "Therefore shall a man leave his father and his mother, and shall cleave unto his wife; and they shall be one flesh."

B. Since marriage is also a civil contract, I want to call your attention to another definition of it. "Marriage is an agreement by which a man and woman consent to live together as husband and wife for the purpose of establishing a home, mutually accepting all the responsibilities which the relationship involves, and properly expecting all the rights and privileges incident thereto." Here is another definition that goes a little further and I like it better; "Marriage is a contract, civil, spiritual, and moral, establishing a permanent union between a man and a woman, involving mutual responsibilities that cannot be terminated at the will of one or both." This puts marriage in its proper perspective, showing that it is a permanent union between a man and a woman, in establishing a home and that it involves mutual responsibilities which cannot be terminated at the whim or fancy of one or both of the parties.

Marriage found its origination in the mind of God. It was ordained for the happiness and the well being of man and was not meant to be a temporary situation. Thus the civil government does not have any control over what terminates a marriage. Even though Texas has five different reasons for divorce, God only recognizes one. (Mt. 19:9).

C. If this contract of marriage were only civil, had no moral responsibility and no spiritual significance, it still would be the most important civil contract that a person could enter. Why? There are several reasons; first, because of the national welfare and security of our nation. A nation can be no better than the homes that comprise her citizenship. Read the history of the nations of the world and you will find that many of them did not fall from an enemy from without but from an enemy within. That enemy was moral decadence; an undermining of the sanctity of the home was one of the reasons that Cardinal Gibbons listed as causing the decline and fall of the Roman Empire. That massive wall, constructed centuries ago to keep the enemies out of the Roman Empire, was never breached by human armies. It still stands today. Rome slowly and surely died from within because of moral degradation there.

Another reason it would be the most important civil contract is because it lasts a lifetime and has eternal consequences. Marriage is a God appointed institution. Adam said, "This is bone of my bone and flesh of my flesh, henceforth she shall be called woman because she was taken out of man." We remember that God said, "For this cause shall a man leave father and mother, and shall cleave unto his wife; and they shall be one flesh." Jesus repeats that in Matthew 19:5.

IMPORTANCE OF PREPARATION

A. I do not know of any venture in the world that can succeed without adequate preparation. None of us would be so foolish as to try to enter into the practice of law without first making thorough preparation. We would not be so foolish as to enter into the practice of medicine without first preparing for that particular profession. The same thing is true in regard to religion and certainly should be true in regard to marriage. If marriage is going to succeed as it should, we will have to make adequate preparation for it.

B. I know there is very little thought given and very little training being done in regard to preparation for marriage. The trail of broken homes and the highest divorce rate of any civilized nation shows that we have given very little thought, consideration, and preparation for this all important, most intimate and most lasting relationship which human beings can enter. A lack of preparation dooms anything, any business venture to failure. A lack of preparation dooms marriage to failure, or, at least keeps it from succeeding as God would have it succeed. Many marriages are held together, but the road is quite rocky and rough and the marriage is not a blessing to those who are engaged therein. Many people will plunge into marriage without any idea concerning the duties or the responsibilities that it involves.

C. Many people have such a hazy, foggy, Hollywoodish idea that love and love alone will solve their problems. They believe that just as long as they feel infatuation for some person, this is all that is necessary. I do not say that it is not necessary, but certainly more than infatuation is essential. There are thousands upon thousands who plunge into marriage each day thinking it to be a bed of roses and wake up to find it is a bed of thorns. Why? Not because there is anything wrong with the institution itself, because it is a God given and God ordained institution. It is because they have not prepared themselves as they should for this particular endeavor in life. To many, marriage is but a legal short cut to gratification of the appetites of the flesh. Any marriage that is based upon mere physical attraction is doomed to fail because physical beauty will fade. If the foundation fails, then the house that is built upon it must crumble also.

D. I realize that God has entrusted the home, first and foremost, with this responsibility of training the children in preparation for marriage. I would not for one moment belittle this God-given responsibility to the home. I believe that this is where the responsibility is and where the blame lies for the lack of training. I know that many homes have miserably failed in offering any kind of training for marriage. The school certainly can render a great service in this regard by teaching and instilling in their students a proper regard for the sanctity of marriage and of the home. Many schools fail along this line. Certainly the church has a responsibility in this field. Much has been written by the apostle Paul telling us how to conduct ourselves in the various affairs in life. I am aware that many say there is no need of talking about these things, that mother nature will take care of it. A trail of broken homes, broken hearts, and shattered lives proves to the contrary. Today almost one out of every four marriages is ending in divorce.

WHAT MAY YOU DO IN PREPARATION FOR MARRIAGE?

We have tried to impress upon you the fact that marriage is not a temporary thing, that it is not something to be taken lightly, but rather that it is to be entered into reverently, discreetly, and in the fear of God. To those of you who are still looking forward to this event in life, there is preparation you can make.

A. First, you can make a physical preparation for marriage. This preparation entails numerous things. Take care of the health of the physical body. Our bodies, if we are Christians, are not our own. Some say, "This is my body and I'll do with it what I like." God says, "What? Know ye not that your body is a temple of the Holy Ghost which is in you, which ye have of God, and ye are not your own? For ye are bought with a price; therefore glorify God in your body, and in your spirit, which are God's." (I Corinthians 6:19—20) "Know ye not that ye are the temple of God, and that the Spirit of God dwelleth in you?" (I Corinthians 3:16) Didn't you know, brother and sister in Christ, that your body is a temple and God's holy spirit dwelleth in you, and that if any defile the temple, him will God destroy. So, a Christian is to take care of his health. Anything which we might do, any form of dissipation, any kind of bad habits, or anything else which would injure our health is a sin before the God of heaven. We are commanded of God to take care of our bodies. We have no right to present at the marriage altar a body which is stained with dissipation, or bent and warped with disease, if at all possible to keep from it. We have no right to expect the other one who stands at the marriage altar with us to present a healthy body when we present one which is marked with dissipation.

B. Mental preparation is a part of physical preparation. Marriage is for adults. It is not a child's game. We need to mature mentally before we enter into marriage. It matters not if you are 14 or 40, 16 or 60 years of age, if you haven't grown up emotionally, you are not ready for marriage. Paul said in I Corinthians 14:20, "Brethren, be not children in understanding: howbeit in malice be children, but in understanding be men." If you still have temper tantrums every time you do not get your way, you are not ready for marriage. Marriage is not for children. It has grave and lasting responsibilities before God and men. You should grow up mentally before entering into it. You think you will marry somebody who is perfect, but the chances are that you will marry someone no better than yourself and then think what this will mean. You will marry someone who has faults and shortcomings and flaws in their character and disposition. So let us not depend on the idea that we will marry someone who is perfect.

Character development is important in preparing for marriage. Character is the only thing that we will take out of this life that we did not bring in. It is going to stand beside us and either commend us or condemn us on judgment day. Paul says in I Timothy 5:22, "Lay hands suddenly on no man, neither be partaker of other men's sins; keep thyself pure." This is essential in character building. Keep thyself pure, morally pure.

C. In addition to physical preparation for marriage, we need to make social preparation. Marriage certainly is a social institution. I think that no one would deny this. I suggest to young people that they should not date those they would not marry. One says, "How do I know whether I am going to marry one until I have dated that person." I simply mean this, there are certain classes of boys and girls, of men and women, which you would not want to be your husband or your wife. If you do not want them to be your mates, then do not date them. I do not think there is a young person in this assembly who would desire a communist to be the mother or the father of your children. Then do not date them. I repeat, if you do not want to marry a communist, do not date one. I do not believe there is a man, woman, boy or girl who would want an atheist to be the father or mother of their children. Surely God would not want an infidel to be your partner throughout life. If you do not want to have an atheist as a husband or wife, do not date them. After the love bug bites you it is just a little bit late for logic and we think, "Well, we'll go ahead and marry now and maybe it will work out." Many a woman has been sorely disappointed when she thought she would take the material which she married and make something beautiful and useful out of it. Later she found that the material itself was rotten and that no man can build a good house out of rotten material. We need to choose our associates carefully. That means that we should not run around with the wrong crowd. If we do, it will lead to one of two things, either embarrassment to us or violation of our consciences. If we say "no" to the crowd, it may be embarrassing. If we are so afraid of being called "chicken" that we go along and do the things which are contrary to our conscience, it will bring about some embarrassment to us. So you are just in the wrong crowd. If you are running with a crowd like that, you have the wrong associates. Paul was not joking when he wrote, "Evil companions corrupt good morals." (I Corinthians 15:33) You are no exception to this rule.

J. Edgar Hoover calls upon the younger people of America to defy the talk of "chicken" and to do what they know is right, regardless of what the crowd does. It is never easy to go against the crowd. Even when the crowd is wrong. Mr. Hoover said that it is not easy to stand up and be called a chicken, but each time it is done it becomes easier. Taking a firm stand when one is young spells the difference between a strong man and a weakling when he becomes an adult. Somewhere, sometime along life's way you must learn how to say "no". You must learn to say it emphatically and mean it, or your life will be ruined and your soul will be lost eternally. The sooner you start, the more beautiful life is going to be for you.

God hasn't set any double standards of morals. I know that humans have. We have set a high standard for womankind and lower standard for mankind. God has no double standard. Paul said in Galatians 3:28, "There is neither Jew nor Greek, there is neither bond nor free, there is neither male nor female; for ye are all one in Christ Jesus." Young men, that standard of morality which you expect in your bride—to—be is what the God of heaven expects of you. Even though society may not condemn you for a lower moral standard, God does.

D. Another preparation which we would like to notice is spiritual preparation. We can handle this one quite easily. This means to be a faithful child of God, not just a church member, but one who does the will of Jehovah God.

DANGER OF MARRYING NON—CHRISTIAN

Now we have outlined unto you three fields of preparation for a very great relationship in life. First of all the physical or personal preparation. Then social preparation and spiritual preparation. Now I would like to teach about the dangers of marring a non—Christian. There are many dangers which come in this particular regard.

A. One danger is that you cannot have ideal home which is divided religiously. No, you cannot. I know you can't. I hope you will forgive me for being so dogmatic, but you cannot have an ideal marriage and an ideal home which is divided religiously. Now those of you who have never known the wonderful fellowship and love and joy of a home which is united in Christ do not know what I am talking about. An old bachelor might argue that it is impossible to love one woman more than another, but he has never known the love of a good and pure wife. An old maid might argue that all men are just alike, but she has never known the love of a good man. Some person who has never known the joy of a united home might argue that their home is ideal. There can be no such ideal home relationship unless we are united. There is no realm in which we need to be one more than in the religious realm.

A preacher once made statements like the ones you have just read. A sister in Christ said, "You are just as wrong as you can be. My husband is a member of a denomination and I am a member of the church of Christ and our marriage is ideal, just perfect." The preacher answered, "I hope that you will not think I am rude, but I just don't believe it." Before long, he was invited into her home for the noon meal. He arrived about 11:30, before her husband had come in from his business. She was preparing the meal, and explained, "My husband will be here in a little while. You know the other day I told you that we are different religiously. I would appreciate it if you wouldn't say anything about the church. We had it understood a long time ago that we wouldn't let religion come between us and so we don't talk about his church or my church either." (You see this ideal marriage situation already, don't you?) The preacher noticed a nearly grown boy go from one room to another. He said something about it to the woman. He thought perhaps this was a boarder. She said, "Oh no, that's our little Johnny." The preacher said, "Well, I haven't seen him at church." She said, "Oh no, I haven't brought him to church. We decided that the father is not going to take him to his church and I am not going to take him to my church and when he gets old enough we are going to let him decide which church he wants to go to." You see this ideal marriage here. Little Johnny was big enough to go to college and big enough to go to hell for that matter. He was living in a divided home relationship. A man came to me from a denomination and said, "As far as my wife and I are concerned we could get along all right, but the children are coming along now and they are wondering why it is that daddy goes to one church and mother goes to another." There can be no ideal marriage as long as the home is divided religiously.

B. Not only is there a danger of having a miserable relationship, but in marrying a non–Christian there is the danger of incurring God's displeasure. The marriage of a Christian is mentioned only twice in the Bible, and both times it specifies another Christian. There is not one example in all God's Word of a Christian ever marrying anyone other than another Christian. One scripture dealing with this in particular is II Corinthians 6:14, it says, "Be ye not unequally yoked together with unbelievers . . ." Someone says, "Does that mean marriage?" If it doesn't mean marriage, it does not mean anything. If you do not believe that it is an unequal yoke for a Christian to marry a non–Christian, then ask some child of God who has done it. In I Corinthians 9:5, the apostle Paul says, "Have we not power to lead about a sister, a wife, as well as other apostles, and as the brethren of the Lord, and Cephas?" Paul is not married, but he says, "I have a right to be married provided my wife is a sister in Christ." Certainly he is not talking about a blood sister. This would be incest, contrary to the laws of God, the laws of man, and the laws of nature. He says that he has a right to lead about a wife, as long as she is a sister in Christ, just like Cephas and others of the apostles. There is one other scripture which shows the same thing. (I Corinthians 7:39) Paul is talking about a woman being bound to her husband as long as they both shall live, but if the husband be dead the wife is free from the law and she is free to marry again, "whomsoever she will; only in the Lord." If that is good advice for widows, why isn't it good advice for single people? These are the only two places that mention a Christian getting married and both times it specifies another Christian. Now if you want to claim to use the Bible as your every rule of faith and of practice in society, in business and in religion, then marry a Christian.

LET NO MAN PUT ASUNDER

A. In verse six of Matthew 19, Jesus continues by telling us that, ". . . . what therefore God hath joined together, let no man put asunder." He is speaking of marriage here; He is talking about the call in society that causes us to leave our own natural homes and mothers and fathers and cleave to our mates for the purpose of establishing a home.

B. Some think that the judges and the jurors of our country are exempt from this command of God, and that it is all right if the civil court puts it asunder. Man does not have any right to legislate in God's realm. When God has spoken, man has no right to legislate.

C. Thus, we could say that marriage is a permanent union of two personalities before men and under God's law. It is a permanent union of two personalities, a complete uniting of possessions, of cares, of hopes, of joys, of pleasures. Someone has expressed it like this, "Two minds, which have but a single thought, two hearts that beat as one." Let no man put it asunder, it is to last for the natural life of an individual. The philosophy of today is, "Go ahead and give it a try and if it doesn't work out you can always get a divorce and marry another." Such a theory as that is what has brought about most of the trouble which we have in our nation today.

D. Every day, over twelve hundred times a day, a judge's gavel pounds the bench and he decrees, "divorce granted". Nearly 400,000 homes a year in our country are being ground into oblivion by the divorce courts; nearly a million children are being left homeless each year. J. Edgar Hoover tells us, "A child from a broken home is six times more likely to get into trouble than one from a normal home." Today we are rearing one of the greatest crops of juvenile delinquents that the country has ever known. The reason for it can be traced back to the decaying and the undermining of the sanctity of the American home. Law enforcement officers will tell you that it is a rare thing for a boy or girl to run afoul of the law if they have been reared in a Christian home.

CONCLUSION

We have talked about preparing yourself personally, socially, and spiritually. All of that is virtually wasted unless you pick out someone else who has likewise prepared for marriage. Almost all preparation will be to no avail unless you select someone who has the same high standard of ideals. Make diligent preparation of yourself and then select a mate who has likewise prepared. All of God's commands are for our good. When we reject them we bring sorrow and heartache upon ourselves and others. You cannot break up a home without breaking a heart.

STUDY QUESTIONS
PREPARATION FOR MARRIAGE

1. In your own words give your definition of marriage.
2. Discuss the importance of preparation in going into business, taking a trip, or getting married.
3. Why is a marriage founded upon physical attraction headed for trouble?
4. Who has the greatest responsibility in preparing young people for marriage? The church, the public school, or the home?
5. Name the four essential areas of preparation for marriage.
6. Which of the four is the most important?
7. Does God have one standard of morality for men and another for women?
8. Name two dangers in marrying a non-Christian.
9. Quote Matthew 19:6.
10. About how many divorces are granted each year in America?

***

Christian homes are but the vestibules of heaven.

When the home is directed by God's Word, angels could spend the night there and not feel out of place.

The time to teach people the truth about divorce is before they get married.

MARRIAGE, DIVORCE, AND REMARRIAGE

INTRODUCTION:
- A. God's commands are for our good
- B. God has made three institutions for man
- C. God is interested in our welfare
- D. Marriage defined
- E. Dissolution of the home
- F. The divorce rate

I. IS MARRIAGE AN ORDINANCE OF THE CHURCH OR OF THE STATE?
- A. God's regulations
    1. Matthew 19:9
    2. Romans 7:2-3
- B. Trial marriage
    1. Legal grounds
    2. Annulment

II. SCRIPTURAL GROUNDS FOR DIVORCE:
- A. Matthew 5:32
- B. Matthew 19:9
- C. "Fornication" defined
    1. Webster
    2. Bible

III. MARRIAGE ILLUSTRATION:
- A. Bill and Sue are married and divorced
- B. Other observations
- C. God is not bound by civil law

IV. ARE ALL PEOPLE SUBJECT TO GOD'S LAW?
- A. Christians are subject
- B. All people are subject
    1. John 17:2
    2. Romans 4:15
        a. Genesis 18:20

       b.   Romans 3:9-10
       c.   Galatians 3:22
       d.   I Peter 4:3
       e.   All men are subject to God's moral law
   C.   Men who commit specific sins must repent of specific
        sins
        1.   What is repentance?
        2.   Can you repent of adultery without ceasing to
             commit it?

CONCLUSION:
   A.   God's law is immutable
   B.   When we break God's law we will pay for it

MARRIAGE, DIVORCE, AND REMARRIAGE
INTRODUCTION

A. I want you to realize that God has never given a command
   that has not been for our good. God has loved us with an
   infinite love far too deep for human comprehension. He
   has not ordered, He has not commanded, He has not
   suggested a thing which has not been for your happiness
   and mine, for your welfare and for mine. And just so it
   is when it comes to the laws in regard to marriage--God
   has given them; God has given them for a purpose.

B. The thing which was paramount in the mind of God when
   He made the human family was to create this institution
   of marriage. It was ordained of God. It was the first of the
   only three organizations which God has made for man to
   enter. In the story of the creation of man we find God
   ordaining the human home. In the tenth chapter of
   Genesis He ordained the civil governments and in Acts the
   second chapter He ordained the church. These are the
   only three institutions which God has made that man can
   enter.

C. God is interested in the welfare of human beings. He is
   interested in anyone's marriage. He is interested in
   alleviating all of the heartache and heartbreak, shattered
   dreams, and torn and twisted lives. Therefore, He has
   given us laws to govern this relationship. We believe that
   an ounce of prevention is worth a ton of cure when it

comes to this particular problem. We believe the only way which we can ever cope with the mounting and tragic divorce problem is to teach people plainly, kindly, and emphatically what God has said in regard to it. I want you to know that no one is going to try to *make* you obey His commands, but I have a God—given responsibility to teach and preach exactly what God has revealed in His Holy Word concerning this plight of humanity called divorce.

D. Marriage is defined as "an agreement by which a man and woman consent to live together as husband and wife for the purpose of establishing a home, mutually accepting all of the responsibilities that the relationship involves and rightfully expecting all of the privileges incident thereto." That is as simple as we can make the definition. Marriage is a many faceted institution. It is just natural for people to seek mates. God looked upon Adam and said, "It is not good for man to live alone." Thus He made a help fit for him. Normal human beings look for a mate when they reach a mature age. Marriage is just natural in the very nature of things. But we find homes being destroyed day by day by one of three ways—by death, by desertion, or by divorce. I know of no other way to destroy a home. You cannot break a home without breaking a heart.

E. Death is the only honorable way to dissolve a human home. Desertion has sometimes been referred to as a poor man's divorce. Divorce has been defined by our lawyers as a legal decree that sets aside the marriage, or dissolves the marriage agreement. Four hundred thousand American homes each year are being ground into oblivion by the divorce courts of our land. Regardless of the reason for the broken home, the results are always—always tragic.

F. In the last seventy years of the history of our nation, divorce has increased over four hundred per cent. Mr. Gibbons, in writing about the decline and fall of the Roman Empire, listed five cardinal reasons for its decay. One of the reasons was the rapid increase in the divorce rate and the undermining of the sanctity of the home. In our country in 1889 there were six divorces for every one hundred marriages. By 1935 there were sixteen divorces for every one hundred marriages. Today there are twenty—five divorces for every one hundred marriages. In 1956 the divorce rate of Lubbock County, Texas, was fifty—six for every one hundred marriages. In 1956 the divorce rate for Potter County, of which Amarillo is the county seat, was sixty—seven divorces for every one hundred marriages. That means two out of three marriages ended in divorce. I want you to know that was a seven—year average. It is not just Hollywo   who needs lessons such as these—they are needed by people like us.

IS MARRIAGE AN ORDINANCE OF THE CHURCH OR STATE?

Let us notice a few things about marriage. Is marriage an ordinance of the church or of the state? This is a trick question. Actually, if you noticed the introduction, it could be neither an ordinance of the church nor of the state because there were marriages before there was a church or a state. It is true that man has made civil laws and God has said for us to be obedient to them. He has also said that if a civil law conflicts with divine law, we are to be obedient to God rather than to man (Acts 4:19). Marriages are made in heaven, but the maintenance work is taken care of here on earth.

A. Let us see what God has to say in regard to the marriage relationship itself. Matthew 19:6 reads, "What God therefore hath joined together" (and he is talking about marriage) "let no man put asunder." This is the decree from the very court of heaven itself, the supreme court of the universe from which there is no appeal. God has warned us, through His son Jesus Christ in the Sermon on the Mount, and in other places, about putting aside our mates. What God therefore hath joined together let no man, be he judge or juror, put asunder.

In Romans 7:2 we find this, "For the woman which hath an husband is bound by the law to her husband so long as he liveth; but if the husband be dead, she is loosed from the law of her husband." "Til death do us part" is the vow which have legalized prostitution, but that does not legalize it in the courts of heaven. The whole world coming together and voting unanimously to regulate marriage has not the authority to do it. The God of heaven instituted it and only He can regulate it. When we stand before God we will not be judged by the statute books of the State of Texas but by the Book of books. It contains the words that will judge us in the last day (John 12:48). I make no apology for it. There are cities in Texas where prostitution is legalized, but that does not change the moral aspect of it one whit. I can take you into places in the United States where gambling is legalized, but that does not change the moral aspect of it one whit. I can take you not very far from here where the sale of alcoholic beverages is legalized, but that does not change the moral aspect of it one whit.

Romans 7:3 says, "So then if, while her husband liveth, she be married to another man, she shall be called an adulteress; but if her husband be dead, she is free from that law; so that she is no adulteress, even though she be married to another man."

B. Trial marriage on any basis is unscriptural. The attitude among many people today is, "We'll give it a try and if it doesn't work out we can always get a divorce and start over." God intended that it should be an indissoluble union not to be terminated at the will of one or both parties.

I read of a woman in Tennessee who has been married and divorced nineteen times. I also read of a man in El Paso who has been married and divorced sixteen times. Think about this for a moment. Those were not marriages—that was wholesale adultery. Is it any worse to commit adultery one time than it is nineteen or sixteen times? If it is all right to divorce your wife or husband and marry another one time, why is it not all right nineteen times?

There are five "legal" grounds for divorce in the State of Texas. They are incompatibility, desertion, nonsupport, conviction of a felony and insanity. God gives only one reason. We will notice it in a moment. In most state statutes there is also a provision called an annulment. I have known some who said, "We didn't get a divorce; we had our marriage annulled." God does not even mention annulment. He calls it "put away". "Whosoever shall put away his wife, except it be for fornication and shall marry another, committeth adultery; and whoso marrieth her which is put away doth commit adultery." More about that in a moment.

I am not trying to keep anyone from getting married, but I do want you to think about it very seriously. I want you to know that the very courts of heaven are concerned about your happiness and your welfare, not only here but in the hereafter. This is the reason that God has made these particular provisions.

SCRIPTURAL GROUNDS FOR DIVORCE

A. Matthew 5:32 gives the only scriptural reason for divorce—the *only* one which God recognizes. Remember that God is the one who instituted marriage. Remember that God will judge us. Remember that the Bible is the statute book which He is going to use. In Matthew 5:32 Jesus said, "But I say unto you, that whosoever (anyone) shall put away his wife saving for the cause of fornication, causeth her to commit adultery; and whosoever shall marry her that is divorced committeth adultery." This is very plain, is it not?

B. Jesus said in Matthew 19:9, "And I say unto you, whosoever shall put away his wife, except it be for fornication, and shall marry another, committeth adultery; and whoso marrieth her which is put away doth commit adultery." So, that brings us down to some terms which have been misleading. (If I speak plainly enough for some who need this lesson to understand, it may offend others. If I speak in such vague terms that no one will be offended, some people will not know what I am talking about. So, I will do the best that I can. Forgive me if I offend you.)

C. Fornication has been described by Webster as "illicit sex relations on the part of single persons". Adultery has been defined by Webster as "illicit sex relations involving at least one married person". Now, this is the common usage of the words today. Thus, many people have erroneously concluded that fornication means illicit sex traffic among unmarried persons only and that the only reason for divorce is for a man to find that he has not married a virgin—that she has committed fornication. But that is not so. The unabridged version of the dictionary tells us that the word "fornication" is many times used, "especially in the Bible", to include adultery and other forms of sexual impurity. Fornication is a term used in God's word to embrace *all* forms of unchastity. The term is used thus even on the statute books of this State. One meaning of "fornication" is illicit sex traffic between unmarried persons. Another meaning would embrace all forms of unchastity, *including* adultery.

We usually think of "adultery" being limited to an illicit sex relationship in which at least one of the persons is married. The Bible uses the terms "fornication" and "adultery" interchangeably. It uses them synonymously in speaking of unchastity in general. In I Corinthians 5:1 Paul, writing to the church at Corinth, says, "It is reported commonly that there is fornication among you, and such fornication as is not so much as named among the Gentiles, that one should have his father's wife." You can see that "fornication" includes what we more commonly call "adultery". Here is one person who is married— "that a man should have his father's wife." In the Sermon on the Mount Jesus used the word "adultery" to include both fornication and adultery as we think of it. In Matthew 5:27 He said, "Ye have heard that it was said of them of old time, Thou shalt not commit adultery; but I say unto you, that whosoever looketh on a woman to lust after her hath committed adultery with her already in his heart." Whether he is married or single and whether she is married or single, any man who looks upon a woman to lust after her is guilty of adultery, Jesus said. So you can see that the terms are used interchangeably in God's word. If you will permit me to inject my definition, I think the nicest way to refer to it is "infidelity to the marriage vows." That is the only reason in the world God will accept for a divorce.

MARRIAGE ILLUSTRATION

A. Bill and Sue stand before the preacher to be married. I ask, "Bill, do you take this woman to be your lawfully wedded wife, to live together in the state of holy matrimony? Will you comfort her, honor her, and keep her, and forsaking all others, *keep yourself to her and her alone as long as you both shall live?*" He answers, "I will." "And Sue, will you take this man . . . do you promise *to keep yourself to him and to him alone as long as you both shall live?*" She answers, "I will." These are the vows made before man and before God. The only reason for divorce recognized in God's word is for a third party to enter into this relationship that has been reserved by the God of heaven for only husband and wife. This is the scriptural ground for divorce—infidelity to the marriage vows.

Now Bill and Sue are divorced for "incompatibility" and she marries another. Society accepts them, but as far as God is concerned, unless Bill had been unfaithful to Sue, she is still married to him and she is living in an adulterous relationship with this other man. I do not know how to make it any clearer. You do not have to be a genius to understand it.

Mark 10:12 turns it around and talks about a woman. So, it works either way. If Sue had been guilty of adultery or fornication, unchastity, infidelity to her marriage vows, then Bill could put her away and he would be free to marry again (Matthew 19:9).

B. Let us notice a few other things about marriage. God's marriage laws are not difficult to understand. He just said, "You are married to each other. You are going to remain that way, unless one of you breaks his marriage vows—unless one of you is unfaithful to these vows you have exchanged." Incompatibility is not accepted by God as a reason for divorce.

C. A married couple lives in the State of New York. Another couple lives in the State of Texas. They pledge their fidelity to each other. Later, both couples are divorced for incompatibility. Now, "incompatibility" is a legal ground for divorce in Texas, but not in New York. At the judgment day both couples stand before God. If God is bound by civil law, He will have to accept one divorce and reject the other!! Anyone with common sense can see the injustice in that. Both couples had done exactly the same thing. One couple lived in New York and the other lived in Texas where the statutes concerning divorce differed. All common sense would show you that God is not going to be bound by the statute books of the State of Texas or the State of New York. God is going to open His book and they are going to be judged according to the things that are written therein.

ARE ALL PEOPLE SUBJECT TO GOD'S LAW?

A. Are people out in the world subject to these laws? We know that Christians are subject to them. People argue that there are two kingdoms—the kingdom of Satan and the kingdom of God, and that everyone in the kingdom of God is subject to the laws of the kingdom of God and those in the kingdom of Satan are subject to his laws.

B. God's moral law is for all men everywhere. I have listened to preachers and teachers all my life who made statements like that and I have asked, "Where does the Bible say so?" They did not know where it said so, but they said "all men everywhere are subject to God's moral law." It is easy to say a thing. It is a little more difficult sometimes to prove it. So we ask you, where does the Bible say it? Let us read a passage or two and I think we can prove it beyond a shadow of a doubt.

In John 17:2 we are told that God gave His son Jesus Christ authority over *all* flesh. The King James version says, "power over all flesh." Then we notice I Timothy 1:9 says the law was not made for the righteous but for the unrighteous, for the unholy, for the sinner. The law was not made for the righteous. It was made for the sinner—for those of the world. It sounds to me as though God's law is for all men everywhere.

I want you to notice now the relationship of sin to the law. Then we will show you how people out in the world commit adultery before God and are held accountable for it. First of all, what is sin? I John 3:4 says, "Sin is transgression of God's law." Adam and Eve transgressed God's law. They ate of the forbidden fruit. They sinned. David transgressed God's law. He took another man's wife to be his wife. He sinned. We need to read Romans 4:15 in order to draw some conclusions. It tells us that where there is no law there is no sin. Sin is the transgression of the law. If there is no law, how could there be any sin? Now we are going to find out if people out in the world can sin—if non-Christians can sin. Do you suppose we can find any non-Christians in God's book who sinned? In Genesis 18:20 the Lord said that the sin of Sodom and Gomorrah was very grievous. They were not God's people. They were pagans; they were heathen. Yet they committed some very grievous sins. One of these sins, named after the city of Sodom, is practiced even today by some of the most degenerate elements of society.

Let us notice another scripture in regard to sin. In Romans 3:9 Paul says, "We have before proved both Jews and Gentiles that they are all under sin." Jews and Gentiles—those who are God's people and those who are not—are under sin. The next verse, Romans 3:10, says, "There is none righteous, no, not one." *All* have sinned and fallen short of the glory of God! (Romans 3:23).

Another scripture to note is Galatians 3:22. It says, "But the scripture hath concluded all under sin." Now remember if there is no law, there is no sin because sin is a transgression of the law.

Let us note some specific sins. In Acts 17:16 Paul was among some pagan people at Athens, Greece. These are not God's people. They were worshipping thirty thousand different gods. The scriptures say that Paul's spirit was stirred within him when he saw this city wholly given to idolatry. Is idolatry a sin? Well, if they did not have any law against it, it could not be a sin, because there has to be a law before there is a sin. The Athenians were guilty of idolatry.

Let us notice in I Corinthians 6:9—11 the different sins enumerated by Paul. He says, "Know ye not that the unrighteous shall not inherit the kingdom of God? Be not deceived; neither fornicators, nor idolaters, nor adulterers, not effeminate (homosexuals, if you please), nor abusers of themselves with mankind, nor thieves, nor covetous, nor drunkards, nor revilers, nor extortioners, shall inherit the kingdom of God. And such were some of you; but ye are washed." Paul told these Corinthians they *were* once fornicators, adulterers, and idolaters. If they had no laws they could not have sinned.

Certainly it is necessarily implied that people of the world are subject to God's moral law. Only those who are born again are subject to God's spiritual law. It would be utterly ridiculous to try to get the hardened sinner to keep communion. It is not for him. He could not understand it. To him it is just a bit of cracker that does not taste very good and a sip of grape juice. But to those who are born again, those who are spiritually minded, it represents the body and the blood of Jesus Christ. There is no need to tell the hardened sinner he needs to attend all the services of the church. He has not been born again. He is not subject to God's spiritual laws. But he is subject to God's moral law. All men everywhere are.

We notice another scripture where Peter mentions some specific sins. In I Peter 4:3 he says that "in times past it did suffice us in our life to do the will of the Gentiles." Then he names some of their sins, such as lasciviousness, lust, revellings, and banquetings. These are specific sins. If there is no law, they could not be sins. Certainly people of the world are subject to God's law.

I think this particular statement is self-explanatory—axiomatic: If men are subject to Christ's law on anything, they are subject to it in marriage. Where is the verse that would exclude or exempt marriage? I am not concerned about what laws man has written in some states. He has given three or four hundred reasons for divorce but that does not affect God any. Marriage was ordained long before that state was ever chartered. God was taking care of it long before that. Do not say, "Oh, it's legal." I have mentioned a lot of other legal things that are not moral—are not scriptural, that are not right.

C. When men are guilty of committing specific sins, they will have to repent of those specific sins. Would it not be unthinkable for me to suggest to you that a man who is guilty of getting drunk ought to repent of gambling? No, he needs to repent of what he is guilty. That is self—explanatory. If you are guilty of violating a specific law of God—sinning in a certain way—then you must repent of that sin and not something else. Would it not be idiotic to suggest to you that someone who is guilty of cheating should repent of lying?

Now what does repentance mean? It means turning from one's sin and practicing it no more. It means turning from it. Just saying, "I'm sorry," is not enough. In Luke 24:47, Jesus said that repentance and remission of sins might be preached in his name, beginning at Jerusalem.

Someone asks, "If I am 'living' in adultery" (I do not like that term because it is not a Bible term. Let us say 'committing adultery'—living with someone else's husband or wife.) "and I obey the gospel, can I be forgiven of that sin?" Certainly so, but repentance means to practice it no more. Someone is getting drunk every day then obeys the gospel. Can he be forgiven of that? Certainly so, but is he going to continue getting drunk every day? Can one continue to commit adultery? Repentance means turning from it.

CONCLUSION
I want you to know that every command that God has given has been for our good. Any time that we violate a command we are going to pay for it now and in the hereafter. I make no apologies for it. Do not be angry with me. I did not write the book. As plainly and as kindly as I know how I have presented to you what God has said regarding marriage, divorce and remarriage.

STUDY QUESTIONS
MARRIAGE, DIVORCE, AND REMARRIAGE

1. What was the first institution God ordained for man?
2. Is marriage an ordinance of the church or state?
3. What is the only scriptural grounds given for a divorce?
4. Will God be concerned in judgment about the different divorce laws of different states?
5. Does "fornication" as used in Matthew 19:9 include adultery?
6. Do people today pay attention to the vows they exchange in getting married? Did you?
7. Are non-Christians subject to God's moral law?
8. Is it possible for a non-Christian to commit adultery?
9. If one is "living in adultery" and obeys the gospel, can he continue in this relationship?
10. If one is living in an adulterous relationship and obeys the Gospel, will obeying the Gospel make his relationship acceptable?

***

If a man leaves children behind him, it is as if he did not die.

Moroccan proverb

***

A successful marriage is one where the wife gives the best years of her life to the man who made them the best years.

THE HOME AS GOD WOULD HAVE IT

INTRODUCTION:
- A. The need for godly homes in the beginning
- B. The need for godly homes now

I. NATIONAL CONFUSION:
- A. Surplus commodities and hungry people
- B. Lack of moral fiber
- C. Public Schools

II. THE HOME AS GOD WOULD HAVE IT:
- A. A united home—Matthew 12:25
- B. A place of piety—I Timothy 5:4
- C. A place of purity—I Timothy 5:22
- D. A place of love—Proverbs 15:17
  1. Mental health
  2. What makes a house a home
- E. A place where God's word is taught
  1. Deuteronomy 4:9
  2. Deuteronomy 6:6
  3. Proverbs 22:6
     a. What is teaching?
     b. What is training?

CONCLUSION: IS YOUR HOME A CHRISTIAN HOME?

THE HOME AS GOD WOULD HAVE IT
INTRODUCTION

A. Back at the dawn of creation, the God of heaven saw the need of establishing the human home as a basic unit of society. The home then is the first institution ordained by God that man enters into.

Not long after God had made Adam and Eve, they transgressed and were driven from the Garden. They begat many sons and daughters and in Genesis 6:5 we see that the Lord looked upon the wickedness of man and saw that it was great. In fact, man was so wicked that He repented that He had made man and determined to destroy him. However, I want to suggest this sobering thought to you. If the homes in Noah's day had been the kind of homes that God would have them be, then there would not have been the flood. In modern history, had the homes of Germany been the kind of homes which God would have had them be, probably there would have been no World War I or II.

We look about us in the society in which we live and we see many things we do not like. We see many things which are unpleasant, but every last one of them has its roots in the home. The society in which we live can be no better than the homes which provide the membership for that particular society. There is much confusion in our nation today. It is becoming common and not shocking at all to pick up the newspapers and read of political graft, moral corruption, chicanery and trickery on every hand. These things happen even among those who have been intrusted to places of preeminence and prestige in our government. It seems that it does not shock us anymore. Those men can be no better than the homes they came from, so we could trace the fault right back to the home once again.

NATIONAL CONFUSION

A. In our nation today we have enough cotton stored to clothe the world and yet much of the world's population has not enough clothing to keep them decent, let alone warm. In the graineries and warehouses of our nation today we have enough wheat stored to feed the world, and yet 60% of the world's population go to bed hungry every night. In our nation's banks today we have more money on deposit than ever before, and yet our national debt is the greatest that it has ever been in the history of the country. These facts may seem a bit confusing on the outset and indeed they bewilder many of us but it is only indicative of the kind of homelife that people have here in

America. A hundred years ago, this nation of ours was known and respected throughout the nations of the world as being the most law abiding nation on the face of the earth. Other nations a hundred years ago wrote about the law abiding citizenship of this nation. Thirty years before Hitler began his rampages against Southern Europe, we find that the nations of the world were losing their respect for America because she had turned into a nation of lawless people; people who do not think it is bad to break the law, only bad if you get caught. This seems to be the standard that our society lives by. I am persuaded to believe that children learn that philosophy of life in the home. The crime rate has grown and increased so rapidly in America that today we have the highest rate of crime of any civilized nation in the world. This is indicative of the homes which the people come from. We are growing numerically as we have never grown before, but organized crime has been increasing much faster than the population. It would be bad indeed if organized crime was just keeping up with the increase in population, but it is surpassing it. We spend from three to five billion dollars per year for education—and I'm for it—but we turn around on the other hand and spend from twenty to twenty—five billion dollars on crime each year. We wonder why our taxes are so high. We complain about this and we think about the immense amount of money which we spend each year in fighting crime and in paying for the crimes of our own citizenship. America, a "Christian" nation we call it, is the nation which spends seven hundred and fifty dollars on pleasure for every one dollar that is sent into foreign missions. Think about that a moment. The average citizen of this "Christian nation" spends seven hundred and fifty dollars on pleasure for every *one* that he spends in taking the gospel into a lost and dying world. This nation has so deteriorated today that the Buddhists have more missionaries on our soil trying to make converts out of Christians than we have in the Buddhist countries. I noticed not long ago where the Buddhists are preparing to build thirty—three more Buddhist temples in our nation. The world has become so concerned that the pagans and the heathen are sending missionaries to our shores! Two of the largest pagan temples in the world are found in America. Four pagan temples are in Washington, D. C. In 1945, the United Nations had its opening session out in a West Coast city. This organization, dedicated to the cause of world peace and uniting men together so that we might work together in peace, started their opening session without even a prayer. And when some of our officials of government were asked concerning this, they said, "We didn't want to pray to God because it might offend the heathen which were there." They wanted to be careful not to offend the heathen people! Where is the moral fiber of American manhood?

B. In Harding College not long ago, I picked up the "Freedom Forum" magazine. Major Mayer, Army psychologist, had come into that particular institution and had addressed the people there on the moral fiber of our country. Major Mayer, along with a team of psychologists, interrogated seven thousand prisoners of war, American young men that were captured by the communists in the North Korean conflict. We cannot say that they came from the slums because they came from every walk of life. We cannot say that they were uneducated or ill—bred because they came from every phase of American life. This is the first time in the history of our country that we have ever had prisoners of war without one escapee. Not even one attempt to escape. Of course they were guarded heavily. They had six Red Chinese soldiers guarding seven thousand American boys! Do you know how many we had guarding the Red Chinese prisoners of war?? We had fifteen thousand soldiers guarding about twelve thousand of them. These men, these Americans, were released after about three and one half years in their prison camp and the Red Cross told them in Tokyo, "You men call home and we will pay the bill." Very, very few of them even bothered to call home. If we ever had the need for Christian homes in America, we need them now; I believe more than ever before. We have today more girls serving whiskey in our nation than we have enrolled in all of the colleges and universities put together. We have over two hundred thousand illegitimate births that are registered and perhaps twice that many that are not registered.

Nearly half a million young women enter into white slavery each year. These facts ought to be shocking to us. It is about time that we quit patting ourselves on the back and talking about what a Christian nation we are and begin to open our eyes to the facts of the situation around us. Yearly we spend:

$30 billion—gambling
$12 billion—alcohol
$7½ billion—pleasure
$7 billion—tobacco
$5 billion—cosmetics
$3 billion—sex magazines

Everything which I have mentioned, and all of it is as distasteful to me as it is to you, comes from the fact that our homes are not as God would have them be. A nation can be no better than the homes that produce her citizens, and these facts I have given you are a strong and bitter indictment against the American home. When I say "the home as God would have it", I mean nothing more nor less than a Christian home.

C. I used to teach in the public schools. After school had been going on for about six weeks, I could tell you something about the mother and father in the home of each student in my room. You school teachers know what I'm talking about. Perhaps I had never met them, but I could tell you a lot about them. In one of our schools, Brooklyn, New York, they have the New York police patroling the corridors. One year we were shocked to find that there had been 222 cases of felonies, major crimes, committed in that high school. Why? The student body of our schools can be no better than the homes that produce them. Just such things have brought about and produced fifty—six million atheists. Now we do not like that thought, do we? There are fifty—six million atheists in our country. These are people who have no use whatsoever for religion. They are not members of any religious order, never attend the services of any church for any reason at any time and practically speaking they are atheists even though they say that they believe in God. As a consequence, we have twenty—seven million young men and young women today who are growing up without one bit of instruction in the Bible. These young people are growing up in spiritual illiteracy and are going to be our doctors of tomorrow, our lawyers, our lawmakers, our judges, our jurors, mayors and our city councilmen. We are rearing right now twenty—seven million new atheists to add to the fifty—six million that we already have!

THE HOME AS GOD WOULD HAVE IT

A. What about the home as God would have it? Let us notice a few things about it. Your home and mine must measure up to these standards if it is going to be pleasing unto God. First of all a home as God would have it is a united home. Jesus said in Matthew 12:25 that a nation divided against itself cannot stand. For a house or home to be as God would have it, it must be united. In no sense should it be united more than religiously. Thus the first prerequisite or the first characteristic of a home as God would have it is a united home, a home that is presided over by a Christian mother and a Christian father. United not only in the bonds of wedlock, but united in Jesus Christ.

B. Then the second identifying mark of a Christian home is its piety. In I Timothy 5:4, you find Paul talking about the children. He says, "Let the children first learn to show piety at home." Piety is not something you eat, it is something you do. It means reverence for God and respect for parents. For a home to be a home as God would have it, it will be presided over by a Christian mother and a Christian father and will be a home in which the children would reverence God and respect parents. It could not be a home as God would have it without these two particular things.

C. Then a third characteristic, a Christian home is a place of purity. I Timothy 5:22, "Be not a partaker of other men's sins, keep thyself pure." This is for both parents and children. It is a place then of unity and it is a place of piety and it is a place of purity.

D. There is another one that we need here: A Christian home is a place of love—l-o-v-e. In Proverbs 15:17, Solomon tells us a little bit about how important love is in a home. He said, "Better is a dinner of herbs where love is, than a fatted ox and hatred therewith." Let us change it just a little bit so that we might understand it better. We would say that it is far better for boys and girls and mothers and fathers to sit down to a coarse meal of cornbread and cabbage where there is love than to live in palatial mansions and fare sumptuously on beef steak and all of its trimmings where there is hatred, contempt, bickering, quarreling and distrust. "Better is a dinner of herbs where love is, than a fatted ox and hatred therewith." The poet has rightly said that it takes a heap of living to make a house a home. It not only needs to be a place of unity, purity and piety; but it needs to be a place which is filled with love.

Home, to a lot of people, is just a place to go when there is no other place to go. Just a place to take off their dirty clothes and put on clean ones, or a place to go when they are sick for a little bit of sympathy or to check in and see how the rest of the family is doing. This is how many of our so—called "homes" are conducted in our country today. We have more mental illnesses in our nation today than all of the physical diseases put together. Our psychiatrists tell us that most of these stem from an abnormal home relationship. I know of several cases in particular where the psychiatrists have diagnosed the case as the home being abnormal and because the child did not grow up feeling the love and the security of a normal home he is now mentally disturbed. "Better is a dinner of herbs where love is, than a fatted ox and hatred therewith."

A few years ago, I noticed in the newspaper this amusing little story that illustrates the point. This particular little boy was checking out of school right in the middle of a semester because his father had been transferred to another city. His father worked as a civilian employee for the government, an inspector for military installations, and he would live in one place for a few weeks and then another place for a few weeks. They stayed here some 13 or 14 weeks and were being transferred again. Since they moved about so much, they did not try to buy a house or rent a house and they had no furniture. Instead he and his wife and child, his son, lived in motels and hotels. When the little boy was checking in his books at the school, some of his little playmates and friends said, "It is too bad that you do not have a home like other children do." This little boy said, "We have a home all right, we just don't have a house to put it in." Someone, in advertising ready—built houses, said, "We build homes, not houses." It is an impossibility. There is only one home that you can build and that is yours. You may build a house for someone else's home, but you cannot build anyone else's home for them. You might break it up for them, but you cannot build it for them.

E. There is another characteristic of a Christian home, or a home as God would have it. Let us see if yours and mine measures up to this one. A Christian home is a place where God's Word is taught. God has always given parents, primarily, the responsibility for instilling in the hearts of their children love and appreciation for things spiritual and eternal. Even back under the law of Moses, in Deuteronomy 4:9, you find God saying through Moses, "Only take heed unto thyself and keep thy soul with all diligence lest that at any time thine eyes forget the things which they have seen and lest they depart out of thine heart all the days of thy life but teach them to thy son and to thy sons' sons." Parents, we have a God—given responsibility to teach our children divine, eternal truth. Grandparents, you have a double responsibility of not only teaching your sons but your sons' sons, or your grandchildren, God's divine and eternal truth. Along this same line, we read in Deuteronomy 6:6, "These things which I command thee this day shall be in thine heart and thou shalt teach them diligently to thy children." Even under the law of Moses, God intended that the parents should instill in their children's hearts eternal principles. "Thou shalt teach them diligently to thy children." Parents, that does not mean bringing them or sending them to Bible study once a week. If I attended to my business only one hour once a week, would you call that diligence? Then another verse along this same line, Proverbs 22:6, Solomon again gives us some instructions. He says, "Train up a child in the way he should go and when he is old he will not depart there from." Someone says, "Brother McKnight, do you really believe that?" If I did not believe that, I would not believe anything in the Bible and I would just close it and throw it on the floor and walk out the door and quit attempting to preach the Gospel. God has said that if we will train up a child in the way that he should go, when he is old he will not depart there from. If he should depart there from, it means one of two things; either we have not trained him up as he should go or God is a liar, one or the other. God forbid the last. Let God be true and every man a liar.

Now the trouble is, we do not know what the word "training" means. You know there is a vast amount of difference in teaching and in training. For example, I could take a group of boys, Junior High boys and have a class each afternoon after school for an hour and I could teach them baseball. I could get the rule book and teach them baseball. However, at the end of the week they could not play baseball any better than they could before we started. Why? Because I would not have "trained" them; I would only have "taught" them. There are pitifully few homes which are teaching their children daily, fewer still that are training them. How do you train them? If I wanted to train those boys, I would take them down to the baseball diamond. This is where they get their training and they might be able to play baseball a little better at the end of the week than at the beginning of the week.

We talk about these things like they are cold theories and abstract notions of mankind. Beloved, they are living principles. Paul said of the Christians, "You are our epistles, known and read of all men." We are not only to tell our children about these things, we are to show them in our lives and in our hearts what they are. They can tell which we love the best! It should not be a contest between God's Word and Buz Sawyer. When our children see us reading the daily newspaper with more enthusiasm and regularity than we read the Bible it is useless for us to tell them that the Bible is the greatest book in the world. That is what I mean by training—*showing* them Christianity in action. For us to say to our children, "We ought to love the church, it is Christ's spiritual body and contains the saved and we ought to support it," and then let our children see that when we want to go fishing or golfing or vacationing, we take vacation from God instead of with God. That is not right training.

Children can see through these things so easily. Train up a child in the way he should go, take his feet and put them on the pathway of life and guide them. I love to take my children with me when I can in doing benevolent work, in teaching, in visitation. I want them to see Christianity, not just hear about it. I want them to know what is expected of them. I want them to see an example, even as poor as it might be. A poor example is worth ten thousand words or more. They learn Christianity in the home; the principle of sharing, the principle of honesty and all these things. God intended that it begin in the homes.

A friend of mine visited a boys reformatory. There were approximately three hundred inmates, from ages 12 to 16. These boys had already committed crimes against society grievous enough to have been sent to this penal institution. This friend addressed the inmates of that institution. After he had talked to them he asked the warden for the privilege of interviewing these boys and talking to them one at a time. The warden was happy to grant him the privilege and so a room was provided for him. These boys were sent in one at a time. He asked them their name and told them his and found out where they came from. Taking a New Testament in hand he asked, "Do you know what this Book is?" One boy out of three hundred even knew what it was! It is taking a lot of tax money to keep that institution up with the guards and the wardens and the clothes and the food and that is just a small drop in the bucket. Only *one* boy knew what the Book was. He said, "Yeah, I think that is a Bible. I saw one one time at grandma's house." That is a pathetic thing, but let me tell you this: for each one of those three hundred boys there are going to be six hundred mothers and fathers answer to God someday for their lack of love for Him and for their children. There will be twelve hundred grandmothers and grandfathers stand before God condemned someday, because they were too lazy or indifferent to instill Christian principles into these boys' minds. An elderly man asked the preacher to go talk to his only son about his soul. He said, "I just do not know what is wrong with my son. He just does not love the church nor the Bible. He is not rearing his daughters as Christians." This man was not faithful to the Lord while he was rearing his own son and now he says, "I just do not know what is wrong."

CONCLUSION

A Christian home then is a place where God's word is taught. Someone has defined it this way, "A Christian home is a place where a world of strife is shut out and a world of love is shut in. A Christian home is a place where the great are small and the small are great. It is a place where our stomachs get three square meals a day and our hearts get a thousand. Christian homes are but the vestibules of Heaven itself. It is the father's kingdom and the mother's world and the children's paradise." Is your home a Christian home? No one can make it so but you. Our nation's troubles come from the troubles that we have in the homes. Blame it where we want to, that is where the trouble comes from and God knows it. God knows that if we train our children as they should go that they will not depart from it. We know if they do not depart from it, the world will be a better place in which to live.

Therefore, parents must set the proper example for the children, walk down life's ways with them, extend the love and the peace and the security of a home to them and many of the ills in our present day society will vanish. This is the only way that it can be done. We cannot legislate moral integrity into people. We cannot pass enough laws to put moral fiber in people. That will have to come from the heart, from the inside. "Guard thy heart with all diligence, for out of it proceeds all of the issues of life."

***

The time to counsel young persons about marriage is before they "fall in love."

STUDY QUESTIONS
THE HOME AS GOD WOULD HAVE IT

1. Give your definition of a Christian home.
2. Has there ever been a greater need for Christian homes than now?
3. Does the corruption in government, business, and society give any indication of the type homes we have?
4. Why has America lost so much prestige among the nations of the world within the last forty years?
5. Can a home be pleasing to God and be divided religiously?
6. Why has God given the home the responsibility in training children?
7. Who taught the children under the Law of Moses?
8. Do you believe Proverbs 22:6?
9. What is the difference in "teaching" and in "training"?
10. Do your train your children in the way they should go?

***

A hundred men may make an encampment, but it takes a woman to make a home.

Chinese proverb

THE HUSBAND AND FATHER
AS GOD WOULD HAVE HIM

INTRODUCTION:
- A. Every institution must have a head
    1. Genesis 3:16
    2. I Corinthians 11:3
    3. Ephesians 5:23
- B. It is not an honorary position

I. MAN MUST LOVE HIS WIFE:
- A. Must love even more than he loves his own parents
    1. Genesis 2:24
    2. Matthew 19:5
    3. Ephesians 5:31
- B. The command is explicit
    1. Ephesians 5:24 and 28
    2. Colossians 3:19
- C. Do you love your wife?
    1. Examination
    2. I Corinthians 13:4-8 (Phillips translation)

II. COMFORT AND PROTECT:
- A. Responsibility of the husband
- B. More than just physical protection
    1. Protection against boredom
    2. Understand her longing to see homefolks

III. SUPPORT THE FAMILY:
- A. I Timothy 5:8
- B. A God-given responsibility
    1. Drinking steals food from little ones
    2. Tobacco steals food from little ones

IV. GOVERNMENT, TRAINING, AND DISCIPLINE
- A. Ephesians 6:4 (Phillips translation)
- B. Men are too busy

1. Six out of 1,600 teach daily
2. The average American father
C. Edgar A. Guest
D. Barriers between fathers and their children

CONCLUSION:
A. Man is head of the house
1. He must love his wife
2. He must provide for his own
B. If he fails as a husband and father; he is a failure

THE HUSBAND AND FATHER
AS GOD WOULD HAVE HIM
INTRODUCTION

A. We can establish from God's Word the fact that the home is a mighty institution ordained of God for the happiness and for the well being of mankind. Each and every home and each institution that God has made must have a head. Any institution that man has made must have a head. And thus in God's divine scheme of things He certainly has placed someone at the head of the home and that is what this lesson is about.

We read in Genesis 3:16 God speaking to the woman, "Thy desire shall be unto thy husband and he shall rule over thee." Then again in I Corinthians 11:3, and I will paraphrase this for the sake of clarity, He said that I would have you know, brethren, that the head of woman is man, that the head of man is Christ, and that the head of Christ is God. Then again in Ephesians 5:23, "For the husband is the head of the wife, even as Christ is the head of the church." Thus we see, according to God's divine scheme of things, that He has placed man at the head of the home.

B. Now this is not an honorary place, it is not a place just of honor, but rather a place of responsibility. If I say unto you that someone is the head of one of the local banks, we know then by virtue of the fact that he is the head of that institution, that he has some responsibilities peculiar to that particular place. And when God placed man at the head of the home as He would have it, He certainly gave unto him some particular and peculiar responsibilities as the head of the home.

MAN MUST LOVE HIS WIFE

A. Man has the responsibility to love his wife more than any other creature on God's earth. Back in the very beginning of time, Genesis 2:24, find that God said, "For this cause a man leave his father and his mother and shall cleave to his wife and the twain shall become one flesh." Someone asked the question, "Do you mean that I am supposed to love my wife even more than father and mother?" Certainly—God answered it in that scripture. Jesus, in Matthew 19:5, said the same words the same expression; "For this cause (that is the cause of establishing the human home) shall a man leave his father and his mother and shall cleave to his wife and the twain shall become one flesh." So, in establishing man as the head of the house I would say that he has the responsibility to love his wife more than any other person. I realize that there are those in our society who take this command quite lightly. Brethren, I suggest this to you, that I would just as soon try to go to Heaven and refuse to repent as to refuse to love my wife more than any other person on earth.

B. Now, let us notice a few scriptures in regard to this. In Ephesians 5:25, God has said through the apostle Paul, "Husbands, love your wives." Well, we all love our wives, don't we? But He does not finish there. He said, "Love your wives even as Christ loved the church." Now we see that He is beginning to put some very strenuous restrictions and requirements on this particular love. "Love your wives even as Christ loved the church and *gave* Himself for it." Unless Paul thought that we should have any doubts in our minds, he reminds us of how the Lord loved the church and he commands that husbands love their wives even that much. Then in verse 28 of the same chapter He said, "Husbands ought to love their wives as their own bodies, for no man ever yet hateth his own flesh, but he nourisheth it and cherisheth it." My, what a contrast that is to some love that we see, or the lack of love that we see on the part of some men for their wives. Men ought to love their wives as Christ loved the church, enough to give themselves for them. They ought to love their wives and are commanded of the God of Heaven to love their wives as their own bodies. Then again in

Colossians 3:19, we find Paul once again by inspiration saying, "Husbands love your wives and be not bitter against them." Now these three scriptures plainly point out how much man is to love his wife.

C. We all would say, *"We* love our wives." Well, do we really? Let us get down to the heart of things.

What is love?As I have suggested before, if I were 21 again perhaps I would have a pretty good definition, but I am more than twice that now and I find that love is pretty difficult to define. It is about as futile to go to Webster's dictionary for a definition of love as anything that I can think of. The Bible is not a dictionary; however, in it, Paul by inspiration gives us some of the attributes of love. Now we have already established the fact beyond the shadow of a doubt that the God of Heaven demands that we love our wives. Let us give ourselves an examination using I Corinthians 13 and just see if we love our wives. I am going to read this slowly and deliberately so that we might give ourselves an examination after each statement concerning love in this particular reading. First of all I would like to suggest that I am not going to read in the King James Version, but for the sake of clarity I want to use Mr. Phillips' translation so we can understand it better. Now, you say you love your wife. Let us see if you do. We begin reading now. "This love of which I speak is slow to lose patience, it looks for a way of being constructive; it is not possessive. It is neither anxious to impress nor does it cherish any inflated ideas of its own importance. Love has good manners and does not pursue selfish advantage, it is not touchy. It does not compile statistics of evil, nor does it gloat over wickedness in other people, but on the contrary, true love rejoices with all good men when truth prevails. Love knows no limit to its endurance, no end to its trust, no fading of its hope. It can outlast anything. It is in fact the one thing that still stands when all else has fallen." Mr. Phillips has put the attributes of love into language which we can understand. It is slow to lose patience, looks for a way of being constructive, is not touchy, is not possessive, has good manners, love can outlast anything. It is in fact the one thing which still stands when all else has fallen. A home which is founded upon love will endure a tempest and the test of time. Do we love our wives? We should answer the question as God has demanded.

COMFORT AND PROTECT

A. Not only are we to love wives, but we are also commanded as husbands to comfort and protect them. Usually in the marriage vows that we exchange we say something about the man's responsibility to comfort and protect the wife. I Peter 3:7 says, "Likewise ye husbands, dwell with them according to knowledge, giving honor unto the wife as unto the weaker vessel." The husband is charged then with taking care of, comforting and protecting the wife as a weaker vessel. The husband as the head of the house has this responsibility.

B. Now then, when we talk about comfort and protection, usually our thoughts turn to physical comfort and physical protection and certainly they are included in this. But any husband that would just comfort and protect his wife physically and let it stop there, is not worth the snap of your finger as a husband. I know men, I believe, who would die physically in protecting their wives, yet they would not spend any energy protecting them spiritually. I believe that this includes comfort and protection from the boredom of managing the home. Sometimes we husbands are just a little bit unthoughtful about the boredom of managing the home. You and I have to keep house occasionally, perhaps, when our wives have gone to visit parents or perhaps are ill. We know that housekeeping becomes quite a chore. I do not mind washing dishes at all if they would just stay washed, and I do not mind making beds if they would just stay made up, and I do not mind picking up after the children if it would just stay picked up. About two days of that and I call for help. Now if housekeeping becomes a chore to me in two days, what do you suppose is the reaction of my wife who keeps the house day in and day out, week in and week out, month in and month out, year in and year out. Break the chain of monotony for her. I do not recommend that (and we will notice more about this further) baby sitters should rear our children for us, but I think this is one occasion where I would recommend a baby sitter. Take the young ones by and leave them with their grandparents and go and enjoy an evening out occasionally. I believe also that the husband ought to be understanding of the natural longing on the part of the wife to see home and home folks occasionally. They have as much right to love their mothers and fathers as we have to love ours. Any thoughtful husband will at least provide, if he cannot go himself, occasions for the wife and for the children to go visit her folks. These are just some things which perhaps we grow thoughtless about which would help us to be the kind of husbands that God would have us to be.

SUPPORT THE FAMILY

A. Another responsibility of the man as the head of the house, is that he is charged by the God of Heaven to provide for the support of his family. In I Timothy 5:8, God has said, through the inspired pen of the apostle Paul, "If any man provideth not for his own, he hath denied the faith and he is worse than an infidel." If you can think of anything which is *worse* than an infidel, it is a man who refuses to provide a living for his wife and for his children. Man must learn, and young men should begin to learn it now, that whenever you marry you pledge all that you have and all that you will ever possess in this life to the upkeep and to the support of that home. It is natural in the very nature of things that the male of the specie be the provider.

B. God has given that responsibility to man as the head of the house. Now I realize there could be extenuating circumstances. Perhaps a husband has a lengthy illness or something like that, but in the normal course of events the God of Heaven charged the male, the man, as head of the house, to do the providing for that household. One of the things, I suppose, that gets closest to our hearts and perhaps under our skin about as quick as anything else is to see some man who will take care of himself and let his wife and children go uncared for. I remember on one occasion out at the farm a few years ago a man came to apply for a job. The reason he gave for wanting to move out on the farm was because he was drinking quite a bit.

He had a wife and three children to support. As long as he ran with the crowd which he was in, he could not quit drinking. He had tried, he said. I gave him a job out there on the farm paying him a little more than the average farm hand received in that community. And we noticed in February when he moved there that the little girls came down to our house to catch the school bus barefooted. Now do not misunderstand me. There is nothing wrong with being poor. God must have loved poor folks, he made enough of them. If it cannot be helped, then it cannot be helped. We noticed, too, that they did not have enough clothing to keep them warm. My wife and mother got busy and made them some clothes, got them coats, and bought them shoes. I had visited, of course, at their house. Sometimes I would go there to give the man some instructions about the work. He would be sitting on an apple crate at one end of the table and the wife on an apple crate at the other and the children standing up around the table. And once again I say, there is nothing wrong with being poor, please do not misunderstand me. That is not a vice within itself. But after he had been there a few months and I realized that he had had time to kind of get his feet on the ground financially, I asked him one day why he did not provide for his children more than he did. He said that his liquor bill was costing him more each week than his grocery bill and he just could not afford it. He had gone back to drinking. And I say to you that a man like that is unfit for the role of fatherhood. He has no right to have a wife and children and God has decreed that he is worse than an infidel. I noticed during the depression days little children asking their daddy for an apple or for an orange. Not just asking as many children do today, but because their bodies cried out for such food. I have heard the father or the mother, as the case may have been, say to the child, "I'm sorry, but we just cannot afford it." Now that is all right if he is telling the truth, but on so many occasions I have seen that same man who denied his child an apple or an orange on the grounds that they could not afford it, turn around and spend ten times that much money for his smoking tobacco for the week. And a father, a man like that, is unfit for the role of fatherhood. By the grace of God, and God is my witness, that if due to bad business judgment on the part of daddy, or due to economic reverses or anything else, that if anyone in our household has to do without, God help it to be me. God has charged man with supporting the wife and the children, and if anybody has to do without, it ought to be man first.

GOVERNMENT, TRAINING AND DISCIPLINE

A. Then another responsibility that God has given to man as head of the house, and one which is almost completely ignored, is found in Ephesians 6:4. "Fathers, provoke not your children to wrath, but bring them up in the nurture and the admonition of the Lord." Did you hear what that said? Let's read it in Phillips. Maybe we can understand it a little better. It says, "Fathers, do not overcorrect your children nor make it difficult for them to obey the commandment, but bring them up in Christian doctrine and in Christian discipline." That helps a little. Do not overcorrect your children. Do not make it difficult for them to obey the command. I have heard fathers yell at little children so loudly that they were beside themselves with fright and could not obey if they wanted to. Bring them up in Christian doctrine and in Christian discipline. No man ought ever to strike anyone else in anger, let alone his own flesh and blood. Discipline administered in anger serves only one purpose, and that is to let the "old man" blow off a little steam. It does not serve its desired end with the child.

B. "Bring them up in Christian doctrine." There is not a father with us who does not think he is too busy for this particular chore. If anybody brings them up in the nurture of the Lord, mother is just going to have to do it because we men are just too busy! After all, Paul, you know, lived 1900 years ago and he just did not understand the problems of the 20th Century. He could not have understood all the pressures that are exerted upon us. He could not have understood how hard we have to work to provide for the family like we should.

Listen, the Holy Spirit guided the apostle Paul and the Holy Spirit of God knew the conditions under which you and I would be living today. He said, "Fathers, you bring your children up in Christian doctrine and in Christian discipline." A preacher, addressing 1600 members of the church, asked the question, "How many of you men have daily Bible teachings in your home?" He said there were six hands that went up out of 1600 people. Then we wonder what is wrong with the generation that we have reared. We wonder what is wrong with the society which we have.

Did you know that the average American father spends seven and a half minutes alone each week with his teen-age daughter or son? Those statistics were released not long ago by a group that is working on the problems of juvenile delinquency. The average American father spends seven and a half minutes—that is one-eighth of an hour out of 168—*alone* with his teen-age son or teen-age daughter. And then we wonder what is wrong with the younger generation!

C. We have all heard the story of the prodigal son and it is a wonderful story, but few of us have heard the story of the prodigal father. To me it is infinitely more sad than the prodigal son. It goes like this:

"A certain man had two sons and the younger said to him, 'Father, give unto me that portion of thy time, thy attention and thy companionship and thy counselship which falleth unto me.' And his father divided unto him his living, in that he paid the boy's bills; he sent him to a select preparatory school, to dancing school and to college and tried to make himself believe that he was doing his full duty by his son. And not many days hence, his father gathered together his interest, his aspirations, his ambitions, and he took a journey into a far country; into a land of stocks and bonds and securities and other such things which do not interest a boy. And there he wasted his precious opportunity of being a companion and a counsel and a guide for his son. And after he had spent the very best years of his life, he had made money, but he had failed to find any real satisfaction; and there arose a mighty famine in his heart and he began to long for some genuine sympathy and friendship. And so he went down and joined himself to one of the clubs of that land. They elected him chairman of the house committee, president of the club and even sent him to congress but he fain would have satisfied himself with the husks that other men did eat. No man gave unto him any real friendship, and when he had come to himself he said, 'How many men of my acquaintance have sons whom they love and whom they understand. They seem perfectly at ease in the companionship of their sons, and I perish with heart hunger. I know what I will do. I will arise and I will go to my son and I will say unto him, 'Son, I have sinned against thee and against Heaven, I am no longer worthy to be called thy father. Let me be as one of thy friends.' And he arose and went to his son and while he was a long way off, his son saw him coming and he was moved with astonishment. And instead of running and falling on his neck, the son drew back and was ill at ease and the father said unto him, 'Son, I have sinned against Heaven and against thee, and I am no longer worthy to be called thy father, let me be as one of thy friends.' And the boy said, 'Not so, not so, I wish it were possible. There was a time when I longed for your companionship. There was a time when I asked for counselship, but you were always too busy. I got my companionship, but I got it in the wrong places. I got my advice, but I got the wrong kind and now alas I am a wreck in body and in soul and it is too late, too late!' "

This pitiful parable is being reenacted in the community in which we live. Day by day, we fathers do not have time, we think, to give unto our children that portion of our lives which we should and which they deserve and which the God of Heaven expects us to give. Fathers, do not overcorrect your children. Do not make it difficult for them to obey the commandments, bring them up in Christian doctrine and in Christian discipline.

D. Edgar A. Guest had this to say on one occasion: "I have a number of tasks to do, all of which I desire to do well. And to be a failure in any of them would be a bitter disappointment unto me, but I could bear a failure in any of them without whimpering if I were sure that I had not failed my son. Not so much of me in the bank and more of me in the boy is what I hope to have to show at the end of my career. For me to be a success as father, he must be a success." How pitiful it is today that some fathers are tied down with their business. When they have a few minutes off they want to spend it away from the family. I remember hearing the story one time of the father who came in from the office early as it was his habit on this particular day of the week to play golf. He rapidly changed his clothes into his golfing togs. As he started out the door his little boy looked up and said, "Daddy, are you coming or going?" I have often turned down speaking engagements at various places, because I know that I must spend some time with those who are near and dear to me.

E. I remember on one occasion a nine year old boy finding a shirt in a store window which he would like to have. He asked his mother if he could have it and she said, "I do not know, ask your father." He said, "Please mother, you ask daddy for me." She suggested, "Son, why don't you go ask him. He's your daddy." The boy said, "Please, mother, you are better acquainted with him than I am." Children have perfect access to the hearts of the mother on the broad highway of love and yet many times there is a barrier between the children and the father. Fathers, I will say this to you, from the bottom of my heart, that if there is that barrier between you and your children, you put it there and only you can tear it down. Do not blame the child. You are the one who built it. How they long for the fellowship of a Christian father. How they thrill to it. I recently saw one little boy nearly two years of age and another in another family about four, who would run from their fathers. Their fathers were preachers, but they would not let the father touch them. They were afraid of them. So you see, there is no one who is exempt from these things which we are talking about.

The Second National Bank in the city of Houston, Texas, puts out a little paper called "Business Briefs". It had this to say in regard to a father in relationship to his children.

"It matters not how sloppy a man's coat might be, how baggy his trousers might be, if his children stand for thirty minutes with their noses pressed against the window pane watching for daddy to come home from work, you can trust that man with anything in this world." Are you that kind of a father? Do the children stand for thirty minutes saying, "When is daddy coming home?" and look for you, or are you the kind of a father that causes them to scurry for cover when the tyrant comes in at the end of a hard day's work?

CONCLUSION

God has decreed that man should be head of the house. He has decreed man should love his wife more than any creature on earth, that he should provide teaching, training and discipline for the children in the home. It matters not how much money a man makes in this life or how high up the social ladder he climbs, if a man fails his wife as a husband and his children as a father, he is a failure. He is not fulfilling the duties and responsibilities that God gave him. He is not a man as God would have him to be.

STUDY QUESTIONS
THE HUSBAND AND FATHER

1. According to God, who is the head of the home?
2. Is this an honorary position?
3. Name some of the responsibilities of the head of the home.
4. How much is a man commanded to love his wife?
5. Is this command any less important than others?
6. What is included in the pledge to "comfort and protect her"?
7. A man who does not provide for his own family is worse than whom?
8. Who has been primarily charged with the government, training, and discipline of the children?
9. Who builds the barrier between father and the children?
10. How can these barriers be broken down?

***

Marriage is the golden rule applied to a very intimate relationship.

***

Marriages are made in heaven, but the maintenance work is done on earth.

***

You may build a lot of houses but you can only make one home.

WIFE AND MOTHER AS GOD WOULD HAVE HER

INTRODUCTION:
- A. Man is the head of the house
- B. What role does the woman play

I. THE PURPOSE OF HER CREATION:
- A. Genesis 2:18
- B. Final and finest portion of God's creation

II. WOMAN IN THE ROLE OF WIFE:
- A. Commanded to be submissive
  1. Ephesians 5:22
  2. Colossians 3:18
  3. I Peter 3:1
- B. I Peter 3:7 and etiquette
- C. What is immodest apparel?
- D. Woman is supreme in homemaking
- E. Nagging wives, gadabouts, and slovenly housekeepers

III. WOMAN IN THE ROLE OF MOTHER:
- A. Genesis 1:28
- B. Motherhood is a unique and exclusive privilege
- C. I Timothy 5:14-15
- D. Just having babies is not enough

CONCLUSION:
- A. A personal illustration
- B. The influence of two women upon my life

WIFE AND MOTHER AS GOD WOULD HAVE HER
INTRODUCTION

A. In previous lessons we have learned that the home is a mighty institution ordained of God for the happiness and the well-being of man. We have learned that God placed man at the head of the house and charged him with the responsibility to love his wife, provide for the home and to train the children.

B. Now we desire to study the relationship which woman should sustain to the home.

THE PURPOSE OF HER CREATION

A. The very purpose for which woman was created shows the role she is to play in life. In Genesis 2:18, God said, "It is not good that the man should be alone; I will make him a help meet for him." God caused a deep sleep to come upon Adam, took from his side a rib and from it He fashioned woman. She was taken from man's side and it is at his side that she finds her greatest degree of usefulness. She was made to be a companion fit for man. Marriage is an adventure in togetherness.

B. Woman was the final and finest portion of God's creation. Everything else was made out of raw materials except woman. She was made out of a finished product. Woman, at her best, surpasses all other creatures in the universe in grace, charm, tenderness and poise. Unfortunately not all women are at their best.

WOMAN IN THE ROLE OF WIFE

A. Just as the husband is commanded to be the head of the house, the wife is commanded to be submissive. Ephesians 5:22 says, "Wives, submit yourselves unto your own husbands as unto the Lord." I Peter 3:1, "Likewise, ye wives, be in subjection to your own husbands: that if any obey not the word, that they may without the word be won by the conversation (manner of life) of the wife." One woman who was having trouble with her unbelieving mate would refuse to cook for him for a week at a time sometimes when he mistreated her. She wondered why she could not convert him!! Unbelievers ought to be able to see Christ in the life and speech of their Christian mates.

B. I Peter 3:7 says, "Likewise, ye husbands, dwell with them according to knowledge, giving honor unto the wife, as unto the weaker vessel, and as being heirs together of the grace of life; that your prayers be not hindered." Our etiquette books are based upon this passage of scripture. We honor women by standing in their presence, by removing our hats in their presence, and by offering them our seats. Some women believe that because they are female that they deserve courtesy, honor, and respect. Let us notice a few peculiarities of some women today.

Some women study English and grammar that they may be able to speak correctly. That is well and good. We like to be around those who can handle the English language properly. It is peculiar to me that women will go to such pains to learn to speak correctly and will then besmirch their lips with profanity, filth, and vulgarity which nauseates anyone who hears it. I know one such woman who claims to be a member of the Lord's church. Her speech is worse than any I ever heard in three and one-half years in the Navy. I have seen sin-hardened men actually blush at the tirade of filth and vulgarity which would proceed from her mouth. I have yet to see a man who admired her for such speech. Girls, young and old, men will not respect you as they should if you are guilty of using impure speech. Please do not lower womanhood and degrade it that way.

There is another peculiarity of womankind. Women in our country spend over $5 billion on cosmetics each year to make themselves physically attractive. I am not complaining about it. I think most of it is pretty well invested. In some cases I might even recommend a higher budget. The thing which is peculiar to me is this: After women go to such pains to make themselves attractive, they smoke cigarettes which contaminate their breath, discolor their skin, and stain their teeth. I do not believe that any woman who smokes is a credit to Christianity. Someone asked a preacher what he thought of a lady smoking. He answered, "I don't know, I have never seen one smoke." I quit smoking the day that I preached my first sermon. I quit on the grounds of expediency. If I had not quit then, I would have quit long before now on the grounds of physical health. Anything which we do that is injurious to our health is a sin according to I Corinthians 3:16-17 and 6:19-20. No unprejudiced person could ignore all the warning on every hand that smoking is a detriment to the health.

Another peculiarity of womankind is this: They take charm courses to make themselves charming, graceful and well poised. This is well and good. Some of these same women will then take alcoholic beverages into their systems. These drinks have an adverse effect upon the nervous system and upon the disposition.

Another thing that we find among women today is an unnatural desire to dress as much like men as possible. Deuteronomy 22:5 says, "The woman shall not wear that which pertaineth unto a man, neither shall a man put on a woman's garment; for all that do so are an abomination unto the Lord thy God." This is the same principle which condemns the effeminate in I Corinthians 6:9. The question always arises, "What about Capri pants, slimjims, etc.?" They are not men's garments. I would not be caught dead in them! Just because a garment has legs does not mean that it is masculine. However, such garb many times falls under the condemnation of I Timothy 2:9 He says, ". . . .let the women adorn themselves in modest apparel, . . ." Goodspeed translates it like this, "Women for their part are to dress modestly and sensibly in proper clothes."

C. What is immodest apparel? It is any clothing that unduly reveals the figure of the wearer. Any clothing that would cause the opposite sex to have impure thoughts is immodest apparel. Immodest apparel is not just shorts, halters, bikinis, etc. I have seen dresses with enough square yardage of material to be modest, IF you would let me cut some off here and sew it on there. I have seen other dresses made of sheer material and they revealed more of the figure than should have been revealed.

If you wear skimpy clothing in the summertime, why? You say that it is for comfort. That is not the real reason and I can prove it IF you will be honest with yourself long enough to read the rest of this paragraph. Common sense and experience will tell you that the skin is cooler when shaded than it is when exposed to the sun. Women who are members of the church say that they wear shorts, etc., because they are so comfortable. These same women make fun of some portly woman who waddles down the street in a pair of shorts. They say, "If my figure looked like that I wouldn't be caught in public in a pair of shorts." Two-ton-Tessie has just as much right to comfort as you do. These same women criticize some skinny woman for appearing in public scantily clad. Bird-legs-Bessie has as much of a right to comfort as you do. Varicose Vera has as much right to comfort as you do. Can't you see that it is not comfort that causes you to expose yourself, it is vanity.

Why do women do these things we talked about? Why do they smoke? Why do they drink? Why do they curse? I do not know. I do know what the psychiatrists say. Our psychiatrists say that women revert to these things as a rebellion against their own sex. They say that a woman curses and swears and drinks and smokes and all these things in an effort to appear mannish; as a rebellion against her own sex and if that is true then it is wrong and it is sinful. God gave you your sex, ladies, and He gave it to you for a purpose. It is not a degraded thing and you are not to degrade it. Women do these and a thousand and one other things that cause men to look upon them with contempt.

I was surprised a few years ago to notice a newspaper article about a thousand high school boys who were polled with the question, "What do you like in your date?" They gave several things, but by far the number one thing they put on the list was "femininity". They wanted their dates to be feminine. Ladies, there is not a thing in the world wrong with being feminine. That is what God intended for you to be. He did not intend for man to be feminine nor woman to be masculine.

D. Woman is supreme in homemaking. God created her and endowed her physically and sociologically as a homemaker.

In Titus 2:5, we are told to let the older women teach the younger women to be sober, that means serious, to love their husbands, and to love their children. You mean women have to be taught to love their children? We will find that out in a moment. They are to teach them to be discreet, how to use a little discretion in dress and in speech and in conduct, so as not to bring reproach upon the church. They are to be chaste, c-h-a-s-t-e, not c-h-a-s-e-d. They are to be keepers at home, good, obedient to their own husbands, that the Word of the Lord be not blasphemed. They are to be keepers at home. We are talking, of course, about the ordinary course of events. Naturally there may come a time when the husband is ill or a woman is widowed or she has to make the living. But we are talking about the ordinary, natural affairs in life. She is to be a keeper at home. My wife is the keeper of our home. Sometimes women have peculiarities in the home that we men cannot appreciate. Mine has one about moving the furniture. If she wants to wear the legs off the furniture moving it about, that is all right. My only request is that she not move the furniture with me in it! She is the housekeeper, she is my companion, my helpmate and I try not to ever say anything about it. Well, occasionally I do, though not often! I remember on one occasion, when we lived on the farm, coming in about 2:00 o'clock in the morning from a trip and I thought I would be kind to her and dress for bed in the dark; I did not know she had been moving furniture. I tried to go to bed on the sewing machine, but outside of that I think perhaps I have never said anything about her keeping the house! She is the keeper of the house. God intended that she should be.

E. Nagging wives, slovenly housekeepers, gad-abouts and busy-bodies in other people's affairs, are the reason so many men seek companionship away from home. I know the man gets the blame for it and he *is* in the wrong. He ought to be strong enough not to do it, but I know of some homes where I would not blame the man for not going home. Wives should busy themselves in making their homes bright and cheerful places in which to live, a place for the husband's ulcers to get a chance to relax when he comes home from a hard day's work. If she would keep her doors open to her husband and to his friends, she would rarely ever have to wonder where he spends his evenings. Edith Johnson, a woman columnist, had this to say in an associated press article entitled, "Why Don't Women Keep Their Men?" Listen to her. She says, "Far too many men are coming home from a tense business world and entering into houses filled with that same tense atmosphere. The wife who complains that the world is treating her shabbily, that her wardrobe is too skimpy, that her cares are too many, and her pleasures are too few, is but adding to the emotional strain under which the husband may rebel at any time. Or, she may demand that he take her out socially when he is too tired to keep going. If our people would discard the foolish notion that a man's worth is measured by the amount of money he makes, or the social position that he attains, then fewer men would go to an early grave." I say, "Amen." We have over ten million widows in our country today whose husbands have gone to an untimely death, an early grave. Do you know how many mothers we have working in America today? More than thirteen million! Do you know how many mothers of pre-school children we have working in America today? Over two million!

WOMAN IN THE ROLE OF MOTHER

A. That brings us down then to the second part of the role of woman. We talked about her as a companion of man, as a housekeeper for man, and now we want to talk about her as a mother. In Genesis 1:28, we find that God has made Adam and Eve and He said, ". . . . be fruitful and multiply and replenish the earth's population . . . ." God made the first man and woman and the rest of us have come into this world through the channels of physical birth. Everybody has a mother or has had a mother. Motherhood should always be discussed with reverence and respect. That is the way I want us to discuss it.

B. As mentioned, God made the first people and the rest of us came into the world through physical birth. I want you to think about this for a moment; that unto womankind is granted the unique and exclusive privilege of cooperating with God in giving life to another human being. This is about as close to creation as mankind can get. God bestowed that high honor upon womankind. Yet womankind today has rebelled against that honor in general. I read in the Old Testament of a woman named Sarah who was barren and how she pleaded with God to give her a child. I read about the joy that filled her heart and permeated the very being of her soul when she found that she too was going to be a mother. I also read of another mother that was barren, her name is Hannah and she prayed and pleaded with God to give her a child to let her fulfill her role as a mother in this life. I read about the thrill that shook the very fibers of her soul when she found out that she too was going to be a mother. Then my heart is heavy when I look about at modern women today. There is such a contrast from the mothers of old. Some modern women think that it is a terrible imposition to mother children. They are so vain that they are afraid it will ruin their figure, or they will have to miss a few sessions at the bridge club or the sewing circle or some other frivolous thing which may not be bad within itself.

C. Listen to what Paul has said through inspiration in I Timothy 5:14-15. "I will therefore that the younger women marry, bear children, guide the house give none occasion to the adversary to speak reproachfully. For some have already turned aside after Satan." I read of people becoming alarmed at the rising rate of juvenile delinquency among girls. One psychiatrist has said that a girl today stands at the crossroads and when she begins to approach womanhood in these very trying and perplexing times known as the teen-age years that there are two courses open. One course leads to a career and one to marriage and being a housewife, bearing children. He says further that they do not know which way to turn. That is no problem at all for Christian women. "I will therefore that the younger women will marry, bear children, guide the house." I know that Paul in this particular case had just been talking about the young widows and the elderly widows. I know that perhaps he had widows in mind, but if it is true for widows, why isn't it true for all others? And if you do not like that passage of scripture let us use again Titus 2:5. He is not talking about widows here. He is talking about the younger women. He says the older women are to teach the younger women to be sober, to love their husbands, to love their children, to be discreet, chaste and keepers at home, good, obedient to their own husbands. Those of you who have chosen the role of motherhood in this life have chosen one of the highest callings that God has ordained upon womankind. The product is far greater, far superior to any farm or factory or business.

We in our society today measure things a little peculiarly. We measure prestige and preeminence and other things. In the Capitol stands a 12 foot high statue of a man called Abraham Lincoln. A master craftsman carved the statue out of one solid block of white marble. As you stand before that polished white marble statue of Abraham Lincoln and look into his face, you can almost see his soul, his character and his compassionate heart. People go there, from all over the world. I want to ask you a question. Who do you suppose did the world the greatest favor, the man who produced the statue or the woman who produced the man? Millions of tourists each year throng Washington, D. C. They come by and view this work of this master craftsman's hand. Not so many go out to the grave of Mary Hanks Lincoln. There have been many plays produced about Abraham Lincoln. There have been many novels written about him, but none of them can even begin to compare with the production of Mary Hanks Lincoln, in the little log cabin, out in the hills of Kentucky. February 12, 1809, she went down into the very valley of the shadow of death and brought into this old world a little tiny baby and she named him Abraham. Which had you rather be, the sculptor who carved him or the mother who produced him?

D. Just having children is not enough, however. That is not all God expects of woman. Any woman with her physical faculties about her can produce children, but God expects far more than that. He not only wants a woman to be a physical mother, but He wants her to be a spiritual mother as well. I remember on one occasion just a few years ago the phone ringing and someone saying, "Mid, there is a family over close to you who are in dire circumstances. Why don't you investigate and see what we need to do to help them." I went over and found a woman with seven children and another on the way. I never saw such filth, poverty, and squalor in my life. I talked to her awhile and observed the children in their rags and in their filth. I went over where her husband was working and talked to him. The woman bought the groceries each week. The first item on that grocery bill was a bottle of snuff for the woman. The second item was a carton of cigarettes for the man and they bought food with what was left of the paycheck. Now this woman was a mother seven times over, but she is not a mother as God would have her. Surely you can see that; surely you can understand what God would have women to be.

I know a boy who was very normal until he was two years old. His parents went out on Christmas to celebrate the birth of Jesus Christ by getting drunk. They left the little boy by himself in a filthy flat, sleeping on a pile of rags. The fire was on and the room stayed warm until his mother came back with her companion. They fell into bed in a drunken stupor. They had turned out the fire and the cold crept into the room and the boy attempted to climb up into the bed with his mother. She slapped him out in the floor and when he tried to come back she finally held him and beat him about the face and the neck with a buckle end of a belt. His skull was shattered in many places. He has been operated on repeatedly. He has a seven inch scar down one side of his head, and the right side of his body is partially paralyzed. How it wrings my heart every time I see him, knowing that up until about two years of age he was just as normal as any other boy and that his own flesh and blood mother treated him that way. Just having children is not all God expects of woman.

Abraham Lincoln said, "All that I am and can ever hope to be, I owe to my angel mother." Emerson said, "Men are what their mothers make them." Even the hard-hearted Napoleon said, "The destiny of the child is always the work of the mother." There is an old Spanish proverb which says, "An ounce of the mother is worth a pound of the clergy." That is the understatement of the year. An ounce of the mother is worth a ton of the clergy. The influence of a Christian, godly mother is the greatest influence that time and eternity will ever know. Statesmen, preachers, elders, lawyers, physicians are all made on mothers' knees. You know, there is a sad part of it too. Liars, drunkards, whoremongers, cheats and gamblers are also made on mothers' knees. I remember a little boy named Timothy. He was a very fortunate lad in that he had a grandmother who was faithful and a mother who was faithful before him. Paul said, "Timothy, every time I call to remembrance the faith that is in you, I remember that first it dwelled in your grandmother and in your mother before you." A child who has a Christian mother is a fortunate child indeed. Does your child have that? Does your child have a mother who thinks first of the Kingdom of Heaven?

CONCLUSION

A. Would you indulge me one personal illustration to close this lesson? April 7, 1923, a woman, living in a not-so-good house on a not-any-better farm in Dunlap, Texas, gave birth to a boy and she named him "Mid". There were four other children besides him. She grew our food in the garden, she nursed us in sickness, her candle went not out by night. She made most of our clothes, she repaired our clothes, she washed them—not on the automatic washer but on the rub board in a galvanized tub—she ironed them—not with an automatic electric steam iron, but with the old flat iron heated on a wood burning range. You know, I thank God often for my mother because if it had not been for her I would not be before you this evening. I am thankful that my mother took care of me in infancy and in childhood. I am thankful that she waited upon me when I was sick, that she fed me, that she taught me my school lessons and gave me counselship and advice. There is one thing, though, which I will always remember my mother for and be grateful to her above and beyond all else; and that is that mother was never too busy to teach me God's Word. Never can I remember in my life going to mother with a question about my Bible study lesson or about the Bible or about God that mother did not stop whatever she was doing and sit down and teach me God's eternal truth. Would to God that all men had mothers like that, this would be a better world in which to live. It could not help but be! You are cheating your children out of the greatest gift which you can give them if you are not giving them a Christian mother.

B. You can blame them or credit them, as you see fit, but if it were not for the influence of two godly women upon my life I would not be preaching today: They are my wife and my mother.

STUDY QUESTIONS
THE WIFE AND MOTHER

1. What was the purpose of the creation of woman?
2. How submissive is a wife to be to her husband? Are there any limits to her submissiveness?
3. How may a woman with an unbelieving mate win him?
4. Read Proverbs 31:10-31
5. Why has God selected women as "keepers at home"?
6. What does "keeping the home" include?
7. Housewives have more gadgets and conveniences today than ever before. Have these things been a blessing?
8. What is immodest apparel?
9. What is meant by "guide the home" in I Timothy 5:14?
10. How important are mothers in our society?

***

The family altar has altered many a family.

***

Nothing demands so much of a man as marriage.

CHILDREN IN THE HOME

INTRODUCTION:
- A. Parents' and children's responsibility
- B. The primary purpose of establishing the home

I. PARENTAL RESPONSIBILITY:
- A. Parents must provide materially and spiritually
  1. We have our children more than anyone else
  2. Must live right in order to teach right
- B. Afraid of making mistakes
  1. We must try
  2. Our children are what we make them
- C. We sometimes teach children to lie, cheat, hate, etc.
- D. Basic fundamentals of living
  1. 1-6 years child forms attitudes
  2. 6-12 years child forms habits
  3. 12-18 years child forms character

II. CHILDREN'S RESPONSIBILITY:
- A. Learn obedience—Luke 2:51 and Colossians 3:20
- B. Must not lie—Colossians 3:9 and Ephesians 4:25
- C. Law of sowing and reaping—Galatians 6:7

CONCLUSION:
You can get forgiveness for your sins but the effects will live on.

CHILDREN IN THE HOME
INTRODUCTION

A. Parents' responsibility to children and the children's responsibility to the parents will be the basis of this lesson. These lessons will be of benefit to you to the exact degree that you use them. Just to be hearers only will not increase your happiness nor usefulness in your home. If we use them, we shall receive blessings here and in the hereafter.

B. The primary purpose for the foundation of marriage was the procreation of the human race. God said in Genesis 1:28 ".... be fruitful and multiply, and replenish the earth ...." Also in I Timothy 5:14, "I will therefore that the younger women marry, bear children, guide the house, give none occasion to the adversary to speak reproachfully." However, we find in studying about the home that it is not enough just to bear children. God expects more of mankind than that. He demanded under the Patriarchal Dispensation, under the Law of Moses, and now under the Christian Dispensation that we instill Christian, divine, eternal principles and truths in the hearts and the minds of the children that have been born into our family. In Deuteronomy 6:6 and 7 through Moses, He said, "And these words, which I command thee this day, shall be in thine heart; and thou shalt teach them diligently unto thy children ...." We find in Ephesians 6:4 that we are to bring our children up in the nurture and the admonition of the Lord.

PARENTAL RESPONSIBILITY

A. Parents have a primary responsibility to their children, not only to provide for them the material things of this life, but also to provide for them spiritually. We know and understand full well I Timothy 5:8 that says, "But if any provide not for his own, and especially for those of his own house, he hath denied the faith, and is worse than an infidel." However, any father who would provide physically and materially for his children and let them grow up spiritually destitute, is not the kind of father that God would have him be. Parents then must accept the responsibility for the training, for the instruction of the children in the home. From the time children are born until they reach the age of 21, they are awake 105,000 hours. Out of that 105,000 hours, approximately 10,000 hours are spent in the public schools, 2,100 hours spent in Bible study if we take them or send them to Bible study every Sunday of their lives. We have them under the direct influence and supervision of the home nearly 93,000 waking hours. That simply means, mothers and fathers, if your children and mine go wrong, we are not to blame the public school teachers with our failure because we have had them in our home in their waking hours nine times as much as the public school teachers have had. It means, furthermore, that if our boys and girls go wrong we are not to blame the Bible school teachers because we have had them under the direct influence and supervision of our home 45 times more than the Bible school teacher has had. When parents shirk their God-given responsibilities, wrecked homes and wrecked lives are the result of it. This is the greatest failure of American parents, the failure to realize that we have a responsibility to our boys and girls, to our sons and daughters, to teach and to instruct them as we should. I have said before, and I say again, that I think the greatest failure of the young people can be traced to the fact that they have had such a pitifully poor example to pattern their lives after. The generation which has lived before me has certainly made a mess of things and the generation of which I am a member is farther from the standard of righteousness that God gave. Our children are what we make them.

B. Some are afraid they might make a mistake in trying to rear their children, so they leave them alone and that is the greatest of all mistakes. All of this talk about the freedom of youth today is nothing but nonsense. I think you will agree with that statement in a few minutes. If you want to destroy a field, farmers, you do not have to go out and sow it to Johnson grass, to possession vines, careless weeds or goatheads. Just neglect it. It will destroy itself. If you should want to destroy a house, you do not have to take a hatchet and break out all the windows and chop up the floors. Just neglect it. If you want to destroy and ruin the life of a boy or girl, a son or daughter, just neglect them. That is all you have to do. You do not have to teach them to lie and steal to ruin them. Just neglect them, that is all. Speaking primarily to adults, we all do what we want to do most. Every action that we have in this life is motivated by a desire. Many times there are two conflicting desires attempting to motivate us to action, and which one wins? The stronger desire. Now it comes down simply to this, mothers and fathers, we must instill in the hearts of our sons and daughters a stronger desire to be pleasing unto God than the desire to be pleasing to the crowd. If we are successful in instilling in their hearts the desire to be pleasing unto God, then their actions will be based upon that desire and not upon the desire to conform. If we fail, however, to instill that desire in their hearts, then the strongest desire they will have will be to be pleasing to the crowd. The righteousness of the next generation depends upon the instruction that we give it. As the twig is bent, so shall the tree incline. Once again, our children are what we make them. The examples that we set sometimes are so bad that I marvel the younger generation is as good as it is.

For example, here is a parent who teaches a child about the Word of God; that it is the best Book in the world, that it tells us about God and our relationship to Him and our responsibility to Him and that we ought to love this Book more than any other book in the world. Then, that same parent turns around and reads the daily newspaper with more regularity than he reads the Word of God. Do you not think the child knows which one you love the most? The apostle Paul or Buz Sawyer? Do you not think the children have enough sense to see through that even though you have said that the Bible is the best Book in the world, the most wonderful Book, the most priceless possession that we have, and you spend more time reading the daily newspaper and popular magazines than you spend reading God's Word? Do you not think they know which you love the most? Surely you do not think they are that dumb. For the parent to say to the child that the church is a wonderful institution, that Jesus purchased it with His own blood, and we ought to support it and then that parent watches television instead of attending its services: Do you not think the children can see which one you love the most? Entertainment or Jehovah God? Our children are what we make them. Once again I say that they have had some very poor examples by which to pattern their lives.

Someone says, "Well, I just do not want to *make* my children go to Bible study or *make* them go to church." Why not? "Because I am afraid if I do, when they get old they may rebel against it and they won't study the Bible anymore and they won't go to church anymore." Does that sound like good philosophy? I hear people using it all the time in the realm of religion. Let me ask you something. Do you make them go to public school? "Oh yes!" Well, why? "Well, it is good for them and they need an education." Do you not think Bible study is good for them? Do you not think they need an education in these things? Reading, writing and arithmetic are fine. They can use them just as long as they live, but the instruction they get from the Bible they will use eternally. Do you use that reasoning when it comes to studying for the lessons in the public school? Do you say, "Now, I am not going to force my children to study geography because if I force them to, then later on they may decide not to study anymore." No sir, we make them get their lessons. It is good for them. Then why not use the same reasoning in both instances? Do you use the same reasoning when talking about taking a bath? Do you say, "I am not going to make my children take a bath because if I make them take a bath when they are little, when they grow up they may rebel against it and not ever take another bath as long as they live." That is absurd! It is just as absurd as saying, "I am not going to make my children study God's Word because they might rebel against it."

C. You know, our children come into this world just as clean and pure and sinless and free from guile as they possibly can be. You and I have to teach them to hate, to lie and to cheat, to gamble and to defraud. Yes we do! You say, "Why I wouldn't teach my children to do those things!" If you are not careful, you do.

A preacher was called into a home by a mother who was a member of the Lord's church. She was very distraught because her son had come in from school one day and had a lot of extra money. She wanted to know where he got it and finally he told her. "We had a poker game up at high school today and I won it." The mother was worried and concerned, as naturally any mother would be, so she called the preacher. "Preacher, would you come and talk to my son?" He made an appointment and went into the home and he met the boy there. This preacher was looking for a particular way to bring the conversation around to gambling, and he noticed a loving cup sitting on the mantel and thought perhaps the boy had won it in an athletic contest. He asked him if that was his loving cup. The boy said, "No, mother won that at the bridge club last week." The preacher just excused the boy and called the mother in and talked to her. Where do you think he learned to gamble? "But this was just a little silver loving cup." Well, this was just a few dollars. What is the difference? I know people who will play cards for a quarter, but they would not for a dollar. Now somewhere in between twenty-five cents and a dollar it changes from entertainment into gambling. Where is it? What about forty cents? Would you play for a forty cent stake? Forty-five? Forty-seven? Somewhere in there it changes. I asked a member of a congregation if she would play bridge for $25 a hand. "No sir, I would not play bridge for $25 a hand!!" "You play for twenty-five cents, why wouldn't you for twenty-five dollars?" "Well," she said, "that would be wrong!" What makes one wrong and the other right? Where do you think our children learn these things? From parents, of course.

D. The basic fundamentals of living have to be taught in the home if they are going to be taught. The God of heaven has said this, and it is time that you and I learned it. God intended that our children first learn parental obedience. It is not particularly pleasant to learn obedience anywhere, anytime or under any conditions. But obedience must be learned if we are ever going to get to heaven. "Though Jesus Christ were a son, yet learned He obedience through the things which he suffered and being made perfect He became the author of eternal salvation unto all those who obey Him." God intended that children first learn obedience in the home. "Children, obey your parents in the Lord, for this is right." (Ephesians 6:1) No child can be obedient to God and disobedient to parents at the same time. The God of heaven has demanded obedience of the child and He intended that the parents teach them obedience in the home. If they do not learn obedience in the home, the next obedience or restraint they will come in contact with is civil obedience. For example, I spent a night in a church member's home and the next morning the little boy was getting ready to go to school. He said, "Daddy, I need a dollar and a half today." The daddy said, "What for?" "I want to buy my school pictures." The father said, "Son, what about those boys and girls whose mothers and fathers don't have a dollar and a half. Isn't it going to make them feel bad if you bring a dollar and a half and they don't have it and are not able to get their pictures?" The little boy said, "Well, yes, I guess it would." His father said, "I tell you what you do, you tell your teacher that your daddy doesn't have a dollar and a half. Then these other boys and girls will not feel so badly. You understand, don't you, son?" And the little seven year old boy kind of bit his lip and said, "Yes, I guess I do." As he looked down he was looking down upon carpet that cost far more than a dollar and a half! He knew that the two airplanes that daddy flew and the nine vehicles that daddy used in his business cost more than that and yet daddy was teaching this boy to lie! On another occasion I remember a couple, both members of the church, who had married during World War II and they were separated immediately thereafter. While the man was out serving his country, his wife gave birth to a son. Upon his return home they were still quite young and had not sown all of their wild oats, they thought. They took up their abode in a west coast city, and it was their custom to go out on Saturday night to nightclubs. They had this little son, of course, and they hired a baby sitter to take care of him. As the little boy grew he began asking questions, "Mother and Daddy, where are you going?" And they kept putting him off and putting him off and finally they talked it over and decided that they were going to have to start telling him something. You know these parents were so concerned that they did not think it would be good for him to tell him that they were going to nightclubs. They wanted to bring him up right, even though they themselves were not right, and so they decided they would tell him they were going to church. He was just a little boy, and that satisfied him for awhile. Then he wanted to go to church with them. They had to then tell him that church was not for little children; that it was just for big people. This little boy grew until he was four years of age and they happened to engage a baby sitter who was a member of the Lord's church. She went into their home a little early and they were in their Saturday night finery and were about ready to leave. They told the little boy. "Now, you be sure and be good and mind the babysitter and do everything she says and go to bed when she tells you to and mother and daddy will be back later." He asked, "Where are you going?" "We are going to church." They kissed him goodnight and went out the door and as they walked down the sidewalk this little four year old boy ran across to the window and watched his mother and father leave, then he turned to the babysitter and said, "There goes the two biggest liars in this town." Where did he learn it? I tell you, parents, children can see through things like that.

God intended that we submit ourselves unto every ordinance of man for the Lord's sake (I Peter 2:13). A child who has not learned obedience in the home, comes in contact with the civil statutes of the land and who do you suppose are the ones that give the law enforcement agencies the most trouble? It is the ones who never learned obedience in the home. They never learned to obey rules and regulations. We find them running afoul of the law. That is the reason Mr. Hoover of the FBI tells us that a child from a broken home is six times more apt to get in trouble than a child from a normal home. After we have learned parental obedience and civil obedience, then and only then can we learn divine obedience. The God we worship has demanded both obedience to parents and obedience to the statutes of the land. Until we are obedient to parents, until we are obedient to the statutes of the land, we cannot be obedient to the God that made us. Are you teaching your children obedience? Somewhere, someday they are going to have to learn obedience.

I have visited in several jails, State prisons and Federal prisons and they are filled with those who never learned obedience. Had they learned obedience they would not have been there. I remember on one occasion going to the home of a member of the church to transact some business, and we sat down in the man's living room. Down at the other end of the living room was a television set. His children came in from the yard and one of them went over and turned the television set on and came and jumped up on the divan to watch the program. He turned the volume all the way up and when the television set warmed up, it came on like a West Texas thunder storm. It just rattled the windows, and the boy's father went over and turned it off and told the boy, "Now, you leave the television set alone." He came back to sit down and the boy met him out in the middle of the room going to turn the TV back on! Of course it did not take it so long to warm up this time and when it came on we could not even hear each other. So the man went over and turned it off again. He said, "Now, son, I said for you to leave that television set turned off." He started back to sit down and the little boy met him right in the middle of the living room floor and turned it back on. This time when he got up and turned it off, he said, "If you turn that on one more time I am going to wear you out." The little boy met him right out in the middle of the floor and turned it back on! This time he said, "Do you want me to get my belt after you? I mean for you to leave that thing off!" Once again the little boy turned it on. That went on for six times. (I did not have anything else to do except sit there and count them.) The father never laid a hand on him. Do you think that boy can respect his father as a man of his word? Do you think he will know any respect for his father when he grows up? That father is doing a grave injustice to that boy. Someone said to me on one occasion, "I love my children so much that I just cannot bear to spank them." I want to say this from the bottom of my heart, I love mine so much I *do* spank them. I used to wonder what mother meant when she got the razor strap and said, "Now, Mid, this is going to hurt me worse than it is going to hurt you." I wondered why she did not hang the thing up. There was no need of hurting both of us! Now that I have children of my own, I know and understand what mother meant. I had rather take the whipping myself than to lay a hand on one of mine, but I love them so much I want them to learn obedience. If they do not learn obedience they are going to lose their souls in hell. Did you hear that, parents? If they do not learn obedience, they are going to lose their souls in hell. The disobedient cannot go to heaven. It is imperative that we start early, too. I know some people who have children just about big enough to go to school, and they have not started bringing them to Bible class yet because they think they are too young to know what it is all about, to know how to behave themselves. I read not long ago in a newspaper about a woman who went to one of our prominent educators and said, "I have a son at home, sir, and I want to know when would be the best time to start training him." The educator asked, "How old is the boy?", and the lady said, "Five years of age." The educator said, "Hurry home, lady, you have wasted the best years of his life already." Did you know our educators tell us the attitudes that a child has toward God, toward his fellow man and toward himself are formed in the first six years of his life? In the next six years of his life his habits are formed and his habits depend upon whether his attitudes were good or bad. If he has a cheerful attitude, he will naturally be one who will be prompt in keeping appointments, and pleasant for people to be around. Then on the other hand, if he is rebellious and sullen, his attitude will be that of slothfulness, instead of punctuality. From the years of one to six his attitudes are formed, from the years of six to twelve his habits are formed, and then from the years of twelve to eighteen those habits crystallize into character. Character is the only thing which you and I will take out of this old world that we did not bring in. Therefore, it is imperative that we start early in training our children.

CHILDREN'S RESPONSIBILITY

A. We have been talking most of the time about the parents' responsibility to the children because I believe that it is the greatest of the two. Now, I want to mention some things about the children's responsibility to the parents. In Luke 2:51, Jesus set the proper example for children. he says that He went down to Nazareth and He was obedient to His parents in all things. Children have always been demanded by God throughout all dispensations to be obedient to parents. "Children, obey your parents in all things; for this is well pleasing unto the Lord." The child who says, "I will not" to his parents is showing disrespect, dishonor and discourtesy and he is rebellious toward the Heavenly Father who has commanded him to obey his parents. God put it this way (Colossians 3:20) as stated above, but sometimes we think the parents are "old fogies" and that they just do not know any better. We say this is the modern age in which we live; but human nature has not changed from Adam and Eve down until this present time. We are human beings just like Adam and Eve. We have the same problems, the same temptations. The same gospel that was written two thousand years ago is just as active and vibrant today as it was then. The children have the responsibility of being obedient to parents. If we are disobedient to our parents, remember we are being disobedient to God at the same time.

B. There is another thought which I would like to leave here, and that is: God hates all lying. I did not say that He hates all liars. He does not, but He hates all lying. He hates all sin, but He loves sinners. He loved us enough that He sent His only begotten Son. Jesus loved us enough that while we were yet sinners He died in our stead; but He hates sin and He hates lying. Now let us notice a scripture or two in regard to this. Colossians 3:9 says, "lie not one to another. . . ." Ephesians 4:25 says, "Wherefore put away all lying. . . ." *All lying*—that means the little "sugar coated, white lies" as well as the "Big black, wooly lies." "All liars shall have their part in the lake that burneth with fire and brimstone." (Revelation 21:8). You say, "I would not tell a lie." I hope not, but be careful before you say that. Did you know that you can tell a lie and never say a word, by just leaving a false impression. For example, in school a test comes along and we borrow the answers off of someone else's paper. We sign our name to it, and we hand it in hoping to deceive the teacher. We have lied. Those are not our answers, and we are leaving a false impression. Sometimes we say words, and the words themselves are true, but they leave a false impression and that is lying. God hates all lying. Who is the one who is going to be hurt by it? In regard to our school system, our schools will be hurt, our community will be hurt, our State, our Nation, but you are the biggest loser of them all. I know you want a diploma, but would it help you any if the board of education came into this building tonight and just handed you a high school diploma? Would you be any smarter than you were before they came in and handed it to you? Then why would you ask them to hand you one without first meeting the requirements? You are cheating yourself. Let me tell you a story along this line which will illustrate it.

One of the most brilliant men that I have ever known was a man who in about the first six weeks of high school went through the textbooks which he had; he stuck them up on the shelf and coasted the rest of the way through. He graduated from high school with honors. He graduated from college with honors. He then decided that he would make a lawyer, so he went to a university of law and graduated. I noticed that he could never get anywhere in the law field. Through the years he would be associated with some lawyers and then dropped, associated with others and then dropped. I noticed that some of his family had to support him part of the time. Finally on one occasion I asked a lawyer, "You know this man, you have worked with him. I know he is intelligent, I know that he graduated with honors. Why can't he get ahead?" This man said, "I will tell you why. It is because he does not hold the truth in high regard." That is just a lawyer's way of saying that he is a liar. He does not hold the truth in high regard. Who is suffering from what? Well, of course innocent ones are suffering, but he is suffering more.

C. Galatians 6:7 says, "Be not deceived; God is not mocked: for whatsoever a man soweth, that shall he also reap." This man I just told you about, sowed unto lying and deceit and today he is of the flesh reaping the results. Had he sowed to the spirit he could of the spirit reap life everlasting. Do not ever think that you can cheat your way through school, cheat on your friends and cheat on your family without having to pay for it. You are the one who will have to pay for it. It will hurt your parents of course, and it will hurt some of your friends. It will hurt the church; but it will hurt you far more than it will hurt anybody else. "Be not deceived, whatsoever a man soweth, that shall he also reap." "Remember thy Creator in the days of thy youth."Religion is not something which you can do when you get too old to do anything else. The God of heaven, through Solomon, has asked that you remember your Creator in the days of your youth. I know that among young people there is a smart little saying that goes something like this: "Let's sow our wild oats while we are young and then pray for a crop failure. Yes, you can get forgiveness for mistakes. Yes, you can get forgiveness for sin, but you can never change the act. You will have difficulty changing your reputation. Our reputation follows us just like our shadow, wherever we go. I remember the story about the little boy out on the frontier. He was like most little boys and got into trouble and made mistakes and his daddy set a keg of spikes down by the hitching post in front of the log cabin. He said, "Now, son, every time you do something that is wrong we are going to drive a spike in that post and when you walk by and see the spikes that will remind you of some wrong deed you did." Of course it was not long until the hitching post resembled a porcupine with the spikes which were driven in it. They became an obsession to the little boy. Whenever company came they said, "What on earth is the meaning of all the spikes in the hitching post?" Someone would take a great delight in explaining that each one of those represented one of Johnny's sins. Finally the little boy came to his father and said, "Daddy, is there anything that we can do to get those spikes out of the post?" His father said, "Yes, son, there is. Every time that you do a good deed without having to be told we will pull a spike out of the post." The little boy got busy, he watched the water bucket and when it was nearly empty he would run down to the spring and fill it without anyone having to tell him. Then out would come a spike. He would watch the woodbox and when it got a little low, he would go out and cut wood and out would come another spike. It was not long until there was just one spike left in the post. The little boy did another good deed and the family gathered around to celebrate with him in pulling out this last spike. They pulled it out—not a one left. All the family was rejoicing, but Johnny was not. His father said, "Son, what is the matter? We have pulled all of the spikes out." The boy looked at the post and said, "Daddy, the *holes* are still there." The evidence of the spikes was still there.

CONCLUSION

You can get forgiveness for your mistakes, young people and old, but you can never change the condition, the evidence will be there. The people who are hurt will remain hurt. If it is the church, the church remains hurt. If it is Christianity, it remains hurt; if it is mother and father, they remain hurt. Profit by the mistakes of others and do not make the same mistakes. "Remember the Creator in the days of thy youth."

STUDY QUESTIONS
CHILDREN IN THE HOME

1. Give one verse of scripture that tells parents to provide physically for their children.
2. Give one verse of scripture that tells parents to provide spiritually for their children.
3. What is the effect upon a child when his parents teach him one thing and then they do something else?
4. What is the most effortless way to destroy a house, a family, or a child?
5. What is wrong with the philosophy "I won't make my child attend church services because he may rebel against it when he gets older"?
6. Where do children learn a lot of their bad habits?
7. Why must children learn parental obedience?
8. God hates "all lying". Name some different ways to lie.
9. Will God repeal His law of sowing and reaping for anyone?
10. Will forgiveness of sin remove the effect of it?

GOD SPEAKS TO YOUTH

INTRODUCTION:
- A. I Thessalonians 4:4-7 (Phillips)
- B. Each must learn to control his own body
- C. Principles of sex
- D. "Passion" is not a dirty word
- E. Hebrews 13:4

I. FLEE YOUTHFUL LUSTS:
- A. II Timothy 2:22
- B. Do not stir up base emotions
- C. I Corinthians 10:13

II. FLEE LICENTIOUS LITERATURE:
- A. Sorry and sordid books
- B. Good books and self-discipline

III. FLEE TELEVISION:
- A. Great time waster
- B. Proverbs 4:23

IV. FLEE MOVIES:
- A. Galatians 5:19 and lewd desire
- B. Movies and immorality

V. FLEE OBVIOUS LURES:
- A. What to wear and how to wear it
- B. What others are saying

VI. FLEE THE MODERN DANCE:
- A. What others say
- B. Fruits of the dance

VII. FLEE MUSIC THAT APPEALS TO BASE EMOTION:

VIII. FLEE SMOKING:
- A. Battle of tobacco companies and medical doctors
- B. Slow suicide

IX. FLEE DRINKING:
- A. The social drink
- B. The results

X. FLEE FILTHY SPEECH:

    A. Dirty jokes

    B. Women and filthy speech

XI. FLEE NECKING PARTIES:

    A. Define necking

    B. What others say

    C. God-given purpose of petting

    D. How to overcome the "petting" habit

CONCLUSION:

    A. Youth is a treasure

    B. Do not prostitute your life

GOD SPEAKS TO YOUTH
(II Tim. 2:22)
INTRODUCTION

A. I Thessalonians 4:4-7 (Phillips): "God's plan is to make you holy, and that entails first of all a clean cut with sexual immorality. Every one of you should learn to control his body, keeping it pure and treating it with respect, and never regarding it as an instrument for self-gratification, as do pagans with no knowledge of God. You cannot break this rule without in some way cheating your fellow men. And you must remember that God will punish all who do offend in this matter, and we have warned you how we have seen this work out in our experience of life. The calling of God is not to impurity but to the most thorough purity, and anyone who makes light of the matter is not making light of a man's ruling but of God's command. It is not for nothing that the Spirit God gives us is called the Holy Spirit."

B. This teaches that each is to learn how to control his own body. We are to keep ourselves pure and to keep our bodies pure from the sins of the flesh. Even a casual observer of the American way of life knows that America is in a moral crisis. I believe that there are at least four possible attitudes that we can take toward this moral crisis. Number one, we can cheerfully ignore it—pretend that it is not there—center our thoughts and our minds and our reflections on some more rosy aspect of our culture than the moral decline that we are in. Of course, this does not change it and neither will it change the fruit of it. Secondly, we may say, "We will just have to condone it, after all youth is youth, and what our fathers used to call sin is really just psychological maladjustment." Thirdly, we may recognize that the moral crisis is real and take a fatalistic approach that there is nothing that can be done. But thanks be to God there is a fourth and a Biblical attitude—and that is to call sin—sin. We must call vice—vice, and to know that even though we might call it psychological maladjustment that it is still a stench in the nostrils of God. We are to expose these things very frankly and very fearlessly. We are to be "instant in season and out of season, to reprove, rebuke and exhort with all long suffering and patience." We are to use the Bible for doctrine, for reproof, for correction and for instruction in righteous living. We are to caution people very lovingly and very kindly and very intelligently about this moral decline and the dangers therein. We are to present the Word of God as the only remedy and the only cure that there is. So, tonight I want to talk to you about some of the things that destroy our morals. These are things that the scriptures *do not* tell us to stay and fight, to pray for strength to overcome; these are the things that the scriptures tell us to flee. There is valor in retreat in regard to these particular things that we will mention.

Last Sunday evening we spoke to you about God's principle of procreation.

C. We said in talking about this God-given principle that every living thing in the universe owes its existence to sex and to this principle. What principle? That there is a special cell from the male that unites with a special cell from the female and they form a special cell that develops into a new life. This principle is true as we followed in Genesis 1 even in the vegetable kingdom, among the fishes, among the fowls, among the animals and among human beings. As we came up the scale, it became intricately more advanced and more personal for with animals it was strictly a physical relationship, but with humans it is more than physical. There must be an affinity not only of the physical but also of the mind and of the spirit. This is the God-given reason for sex. We noticed also that the sex urge is normal; just as normal as the urge to eat. When boys and girls reach the age of puberty or the age when they are changing from boys and girls into men and women, there is a pituitary gland at the base of the brain that begins to manufacture chemicals that we call sex hormones. Certain portions of the body respond to these sex hormones and begin to grow and develop, and the boys and girls become interested in each other. This urge is just as natural and just as normal and just as holy and just as pure as any other God-given urge.

D. The word "passion" is not a dirty word. It simply means the normal appetite of the flesh. But we also discovered in our lesson last Sunday evening that the only legitimate, the only moral place for the gratification of this urge is inside of marriage. God never condemns this sex urge nor the gratification of it as long as it is inside the bonds of holy wedlock. It is only the abuse of this urge and the abuse of this appetite that God condemns.

E. We read in Hebrews 13:4 that marriage is honorable in all and the bed is not defiled. In Phillips translation this same scripture reads, "both honorable marriage and chastity should be respected by all of you. God himself will judge those of you who traffic in the bodies of others or who defile the relationship of marriage." Marriage is given of God for a high and holy purpose. There is nothing wrong with this purpose as long as it is within the bonds of wedlock. We have, however, many traps along life's way that ensnare us. Paul said we are not ignorant of Satan's devices (II Cor. 2:11). Satan goeth about as a roaring lion seeking whom he may devour. We are not ignorant of his devices. It is to instruct you in regard to his devices that I bring this lesson to you this evening.

FLEE YOUTHFUL LUSTS

A. There are many things that we are to flee. I think I will take as a scripture text for the rest of the sermon II Timothy 2:22—three words—"flee youthful lust." "Flee youthful lust." I like the way some of the modern language translations translate this. The New English version says this. "Turn away from the wayward impulses of youth." Williams translates it like this. "You must keep on fleeing the evil desires and the impulses of youth." Phillips translates it like this. "Turn your back on the turbulent desires of youth." Joseph did. Joseph, a choice young man, had a very immoral woman who came to him with a very immoral proposition and he said, "I will not sin"—against me? No, he did not say that. "I will not sin against your husband." He did not say that. "I will not sin against you." No, he said, "I will not sin against my God and do this thing." All of the Josephs are not dead, thank God. I know of some of them in this audience tonight—men of virtue, men of character such as Joseph was. The reason for the warnings and the reason for the sermon is simply that physical intimacy between two people who are not married to each other is the most dangerous thing in the world. You have no right to stir up desires which you have no right to fulfill and to satisfy.

B. Jesus said, "Ye have heard it said of them of old time, Thou shalt not murder. But I say unto you, ye shall not even hate." Why? Because hatred produces murder, that is why. Then a few verses later, He forbade us to even say, "Thou fool" to our neighbor. Why? Because to say "thou fool" produces hate and hatred produces murder. Jesus knew that it was not only wrong to murder, but it was wrong to incite the desires to murder. Then in the same regard, He said, "Thou shalt not commit adultery." He continued by saying, "Thou shalt not stir up the desires that cause you to commit adultery." You have, then, no legitimate right to stir up desires within your body which you have no right to consummate or to fulfill.

C. There are certain things which you and I must learn to flee. Let us notice a few of them. In regard to the temptations that come our way, we notice first of all in I Cor. 10:13 that with every temptation God will send a way of escape. He has promised it, we have to look for it; and if you cannot find it any other way, get down on your knees and search for it. Perhaps you can find it there. Then in verse 14, if I may stop in the middle of the sentence, the writer says, "Wherefore, beloved brethren, flee. . . ." We will stop right there because that is the only way to handle some of the temptations, simply flee. In I Cor. 6:18, two words, "flee fornication." Another scripture given in I Timothy 6:11, Paul is writing to Timothy. He is writing to a young man who felt the same urges and the same impulses you feel. He had the same temptations which you have. It was a very licentious life that was ordinarily lived in the Roman Empire, and Paul writes to him and says, "But thou, O man of God, flee these things." This is one time when it is not wise to stand and fight. It is wiser to run, to flee as Joseph did even if he left his coat in the hands of the woman who had made the amorous advances toward him. Flee these things. Now then, what things shall we flee?

FLEE LICENTIOUS LITERATURE

A. I am going to name at least ten things that destroy morals of people young and old. Number one that I will mention is: flee licentious literature. There is a lot of it. There are a lot of books that are not only cheap, money-wise, but they are cheap in content. These are books that will poison the mind. They are sorry and sordid. You are now, or you are rapidly becoming that which you read. Whatever you take into your mind is going to make you what you are. So, if you continue to digest filth in your mind, you are going to develop into a filthy person. "Whatsoever a man soweth, that shall he also reap." There are just no two ways about it.

B. I know that just as assuredly as there is licentious literature on every hand available to high school, junior high, or any one that can read here in this city and other cities as well, that there is also good material which you can read. Christian book stores throughout the land stock good books. Books which appeal not to the baser part of a person, not to the things which would drag you down, but to the things which elevate you. I know this. It is not quite as sensational to read the good books as to read the other kind; but the Christian life demands self discipline. We must learn to master our own bodies and we are to tell ourselves and our bodies what we shall read and not let the flesh dictate to us. I would suggest to you, then, flee licentious literature.

what we shall read and not let the flesh dictate to us. I would suggest to you, then, flee licentious literature.

FLEE TELEVISION

A. The next thing I would suggest in fleeing these things, is this. Flee television. It tempts you, first of all, to waste your life. Many of you could say, as a young man once said, "I used to come in from school and get my home work, then I had time to play for a while, read a couple of chapters in the Bible, then pray before I went to bed. But now, since we brought television into the house, I come in and I fall into the chair and I begin to watch one program and then another and the first thing I know it is bed time and I haven't gotten my home work, my grades are slipping, I haven't time to read the Bible and I fall into bed tired at night." It not only tempts you to waste your time, but it tempts you to degrade and defile your life, because there is much on television that is obscene filth. Whenever you feed your heart and your mind upon this sort of thing, you are going to become like the things which you are seeing and hearing. You just cannot help it.

B. Proverbs 4:23 says, "Guard thy heart with all diligence." Why? because "out of the heart proceeds all the issues of life." If you put the wrong things into the heart, the wrong things are going to come out of the heart. Listen to Him in Matthew 15:19, "For out of the heart comes evil thoughts, murders, adulteries, fornication, false witness, thefts, blasphemy. These are the things which defile a man." Out of the heart comes these things. What puts them in there? What we see and what we hear. Now radio and television are like a knife. They can be used rightly or wrongly. I gave one of my little boys a knife recently and I taught him how to use it rightly. There is a lot of good that can be had from television and from radio. I am not condemning everything which is on them, but I do know that there is a lot that is obscene filth and trash and I know that you are tempted to feast upon this with your eyes and with your ears. You cannot do it without it coloring and shaping your life and your soul as well.

FLEE MOVIES

A. Flee movies which tend to produce lewd desires. I think it would be well to insert a scripture here, Gal. 5:19, the King James Version reads like this, "But the works of the flesh which are manifest are these; adultery, fornication, uncleanness and lasciviousness." What is lasciviousness? It is anything which tends to produce an evil impulse — anything which tends to produce a lewd desire. These are sex traps. So, I say flee movies which cater to the immoral. Is there any other kind? If so, they are pretty rare specimens and they are getting fewer all the time. I can remember as a boy that parents did not have to worry about their children going to a "western" because in the first place the hero always wore a white hat and rode a white horse which were symbols of his purity and virtue. Not only that, he was always kind to his horse and to women too. He never drank anything stronger than buttermilk. He was never guilty of profanity. He did not smoke. As a matter of fact, about the only thing we could find wrong was in the last few seconds when he kissed the leading lady. We found it very nauseating, so we closed our eyes! We tried to forgive him for it!!

B. Today that is not the case and you know it. Hollywood and other movie centers are catering to the immoral and they try to portray and depict immorality of all kinds as being normal. There are the sex queens of Hollywood who thrill people and try to lead you off into imitations of them. I believe that perhaps Hollywood produced movies have done more to defile the youth of our land than any other one thing. I refer to such movies as those that would make a call girl the heroine; such movies as one that used a sex pervert as the leading character and try to portray immorality as normal and natural. Whenever a movie like this comes to town all you have to do is drive by and you will see college and high school students lined up for two or three blocks to buy tickets. These are the things which appeal to the baser emotions of an individual. These are things which are wrong. These are things which will lead you off into sin, farther and farther away from God. J John 3:3 has this to say. "Every man that has this hope, purifieth himself even as he is pure." What you see, what you hear, what you read, what you engage in will be what you will become. You are just not good enough to say that it will not have any effect on me and it will not rub off, because it will.

FLEE OBVIOUS LURES

A. Our Hollywood starlets are usually very beautiful—physically. Not only that, but they are wealthy and they can afford to dress themselves attractively. They are usually held up as examples to the young ladies. There arises a question in the minds of many young girls who would like to be Christians. Can I dress like them and be a Christian? Can I wear clothes as fittingly provocative as they and be a Christian? Unfortunately, the answer to the question is not as simple as, "Don't wear Capri pants—do wear cotton stockings." The answer depends not only upon *what* you wear, but *how* you wear it. Two girls can wear exactly the same dress, and one can be very modestly clad and the other very immodestly clad. A priest said, "Girls, watch your sweater bait." Crude, isn't it? But you know what he is talking about. If you dress so as to accentuate the body, you had better look out. If your clothing accentuates the body, your figure, if your clothing says "come on," you are going to attract a certain type of man. Why do you dress like you do? To call attention to the body. You are headed for trouble. You are going to hurt somebody and it may be you who gets hurt.

B. Let us notice an article or two in regard to the attire. The following article was written by a high school teacher in another state. "We teachers have tried to set some standards of dress, but so many parents complained that the Board of Education would not uphold us. In our high school, over half the girls come to classes in everything from the shortest shorts to the tightest of tight stretch pants. I have had girls in my classes for nine months, five days a week, whom I have never seen in a dress. High school boys are not mature enough to control emotions stirred up by the sight of all this nakedness and revealing outlines of feminine figures. It is no wonder more and more high school girls are forced to leave school because of pregnancy. If mothers could see how their daughters behave in un-lady-like dress, they would not let them out of the door." A quarter of a million high school girls leave their school desks each year and head for the maternity wards. One out of every eight babies born in the United States is born outside of wedlock today. That is the reason that I talk to you about these particular things. I would say then, flee these obvious lures. In I Thes. 5:22, listen to Paul, "Abstain from the very appearance of evil." Do not think that you can dress so as to stir the passions of man and then say, "Well, it was not my fault." Jesus said that if you cause your fellowman to stumble you are just as guilty as he and it would be better for you to have a millstone hanged about your neck and drowned in the depths of the sea than to cause one of your fellowmen to lose his way from earth to heaven. Here is a report from a fellow who lost a six-year old daughter to a sex maniac. Perhaps some of you read about this in the paper. I take these words from the reporters. He said, "I do not blame the man as much as I blame the society that produces the men. It is such a society that allows sex magazines on the stands for our kids to read. A society that measures Hollywood stars by their bosoms. A society where the telling of dirty stories and the use of foul language is common place. These things produce sex perverts out of people who have even the slightest abnormal tendencies. They are encouraged by everything around them, and until society changes its fundamental moral precepts and reasserts a belief in God, we shall continue to have sex perverts." We say, "let's get rid of these things" and then we turn right around and do the very thing that fosters them.

FLEE THE MODERN DANCE

A. If you want to remain pure, flee the modern dance. Here is a quotation from a Mrs. Henryetta Hunt. She is the superintendent of Springfield, Illinois, Redemption Home. She says, "Dancing drags down more girls than any thing else. Fully half of those who came to us last year went wrong at the public school dances right here in Springfield." Another is from Miss Clara Jones. She is a field worker for the North Dakota House of Mercy. She says that "75 to 90 percent of those who slipped over the edge and slid into sex sin and entered unmarried motherhood at the North Dakota House of Mercy, tell one single story—the modern dance." What is wrong with dancing? I can answer it very easily. You are too close physically. You say, "we are not as close physically dancing as doing something else." I am going to get to that "something else" in a few minutes.

B. The last time I preached on dancing here was about two years ago. After the service was dismissed, a 16 year old, unwed, expectant mother said, "Brother McKnight, if I had learned that lesson six months ago, I would not be in this condition." There is many a girl now who could not see a thing in the world wrong with it when they started. Flee the modern dance.

FLEE MUSIC THAT APPEALS TO BASER EMOTIONS

You may call it "rock-n-roll" or whatever you want, but music which appeals to the baser emotions of man is not good for you. Nothing wrong with it? My files are bulging with newspaper clippings of riots that have ensued, of 73 policemen being called out to stop a dance which got out of hand, of $3,000 damage which rock-n-rollers did to one ballroom and such things as that because they lost control of themselves. Flee this kind of music. There is a lot of good music in the world to take the place of this kind.

FLEE SMOKING

A. If you have started smoking or not, shun it like the plague. Now why do I say that? That little round, thin cigarette has become a modern battleground for the bodies of men, women, boys and girls. On one hand drawn up in dread array are the tobacco growers and the tobacco companies intending to keep making a profit. Over on the other hand is the medical profession which is becoming increasingly alarmed over the early death rate for smokers. Here are some statistics for you. If you smoke up to a half pack a day, just a half pack a day, you increase your chances of dying of lung cancer fifteen times. I was in a certain city recently where a famous surgeon and physician came and spoke to a civic club there on the subject of smoking. He gave them a lot of fancy figures. Then he finally said, "Now, fellows, I am going to put this down where you can understand. I am going to reduce it down to a very cold, mathematical formula so that you can understand what I am talking about. It has been proven by thousands of doctors, and multiplied thousands of smokers, that every pack of cigarettes you smoke takes one day off of your life." Now, I want to ask you something. Is it worse to commit suicide in 20 seconds than it is to take 20 years? I think we all agree that no man or woman has a right to take his or her own life. What is the difference if you take it in 20 seconds or you take it over a period of 20 years?

B. A lifelong acquaintance of mine is now dying of lung cancer. He used to be an elder in the church. I can remember him with a cigarette between his fingers, almost everywhere that I saw him. He still could have had years of usefulness. You are not your own; you are bought with a price. That price is the blood of Christ. "Know ye not that ye are the temple of God, and that the Spirit of God dwelleth in you?" (I Cor. 3:16-17). Your body is the temple of God and if any man will defile the temple, him will God destroy. Why don't people quit smoking? I will tell you why—because they cannot. They would if they could. Of course, someone who is just getting started and still thinks it is smart and cute, does not want to quit yet. But I am talking about those who are addicted to the habit, they cannot quit. *Cannot* quit. I quit smoking 12 years ago. I have had hundreds upon hundreds of cigarettes offered me since that time and I have refused every one of them, and I have yet to find anyone who would say, "Oh, you poor fellow, you don't smoke?" Time and time again, they will say, "You don't smoke? You are lucky." It is not luck. I used to smoke two packs a day, regularly. It is not luck. The reason that people can't quit is because the smoke contains nicotine and nicotine is a drug and the body becomes addicted to it. They have accustomed their bodies to receiving so much nicotine each day and when you take it away the nerves get frayed and taut. I feel sorry for the man or woman who is trying to quit, but I sympathize more deeply with their associates, because they will become pretty short on temper. It is rough. I know that it is. One of my children asked the other day, "Daddy, what is smoking good for anyway besides to give you lung cancer?" I said, "Why, it is good for a lot of things. It will contaminate your breath, stain your teeth, and discolor your skin. It will cause you to have an obnoxious odor among those that do not smoke." It is good for a lot of things, you see. A teen-age boy starts smoking. Why? For one reason alone, and that is to prove he is a man. Now, you boys know this is right. It makes you feel smart and sophisticated. You see so many pictures in magazines and so many ads of very sophisticated people smoking, that it just makes you feel important and makes you feel grown up. You want to prove you are a man and this is the reason you start and 30 years later you will be trying to quit to prove the same thing. Well, what has this got to do with our morals? Because you are catering to a desire of the flesh. Because you are weakening your own moral fiber, any time that you do this. So, I would say, flee smoking.

FLEE DRINKING

A. A social drink won't hurt you? Notice this letter from a GI who is now serving in Japan. "As you know, I am in the military police and the power of Satan is strong here in Japan. These GIs need to know of the gospel of Christ. They fear nothing and some day they will be suffering for their sins. Drink here is so common that most GIs drink every night until they are broke and then they will put some of their clothes in the pawn shop to get money to go out and get drunk and spend the night with some Japanese girl. Opium seems to be one of the main products in Japan, and our GIs are sure buying it up. I am afraid that the United States is falling quickly and God is going to punish her for her sins. If only the Christians in the United States knew what goes on here, they would be more on fire for Christ. I am a GI missionary serving my Lord in Japan." Over and over and over again the lie is told, "A social drink won't hurt you." Of course, this is the beginning, because the social drinker develops into a moderate drinker and the moderate drinker into a heavy drinker and the heavy drinker into a problem drinker and the problem drinker into an alcoholic so that we have nearly one-third of a million alcoholics in this State of Texas today, who cost us over fifty million dollars a year. We are producing alcoholics in the United States at the rate of twelve hundred a day, and we now have six million of them. No one ever takes that first social drink intending to turn out to be a drunkard. You can call them alcoholics if you want, but I call them what they are, drunkards. There are six million of them in the country in which we live. Someone says, "Oh, he had one drink too many." If he had his first one, he had one too many. If you do not ever take that first one, you don't have to worry about these problems.

B. Flee these things. Cirrhosis of the liver is the fifth most frequent cause of death in our country. Just being a moderate drinker increases your chances of dying with this disease seven times. It is detrimental to your health, just like smoking is. Flee these things. The social drink has been the downfall of many a young person, because it does not take much alcohol to anesthetize the conscience and to paralyze the will. The things which would be abhorrent to you sober, become pretty attractive to you while you are drunk or under the influence of drink. One boy in Fort Worth boasted that if he could get a girl to take two drinks with him and dance with him, he could take liberties with her when he wanted to. He knew what he was talking about. I suppose that is the reason that some one came up with the terse little verse, "Candy is dandy, but liquor is quicker." You know that it causes you to have base emotions and to lose self-control. If you have ever drunk anything, you know that. That is the reason that when the fellow stopped at the moonshiners to buy some liquor, the moonshiner said, "What kind of liquor do you want?" The fellow said, "What do you mean, what kind?" The moonshiner replied, "Courting liquor, or fighting liquor." These are the two emotions that it appeals to in man. This is the reason so many people commit sins under the influence of drink which they would not even think of if they were sober; so I say to you, flee alcoholic drink.

FLEE FILTHY SPEECH

A. I know that sex and the relation between the sexes has been the butt end of a lot of filthy obscenities. I know that this lowers our respect for this God-given union which was established to bring two people together in the closest, intimate, most tender of all human relationships for the purpose of creating a mind, a spirit, and a body in their likeness and in the likeness of God. To laugh and to joke and to jest about something which is that pure and holy shows a crassness of spirit, a crudeness of soul. Many a married man has found this out. He has said, "You know, sex used to be ugly and I used to jest and joke about it and then I got married to the finest girl in the world, and in the process of time I had to take her to the hospital for the birth of our first child. I have stood by her bedside when she was in labor, paying for the sin of Eve. I loved her so much that I would have taken her place if I could. I have seen her go down into the very valley of the shadow of death to produce a human being in my image. Then like a flash it came to my mind what sex is all about and I have been ashamed of my irreverence and I have wept."

B. It is only recently that women in this country have begun to joke, at least publicly, about sex and to tell filthy, dirty stories about this God-given, holy relationship. For a woman to have, in union with God, the power of creation in her body and then to joke about it shows that she is dirty and filthy. Boys, girls, men and women you cannot live with dirt and not get dirty. If your speech is ugly, it means your heart is ugly and your soul is ugly. To any woman who would joke about God's law of procreation, I say that you may be just as beautiful as a dream walking; but deep down inside your soul, you are dirty and ugly and vile and vulgar. You may be as pretty as a picture, but you are ugly inside. You know why mankind does not respect you any more. As long as woman was up there on that pedestal where God put her, she was always reaching down and lifting man up, lifting him up out of his barbarities, out of his ugliness, out of his harshness; but then came equal rights and womankind came down where man is and now he does all that he can to destroy whatever virtues she has. He has no respect for her. If you want to elevate the world's morals, then women, get up there on that pedestal where God put you, and lift man up there too. Flee filthy speech.

FLEE NECKING PARTIES

A. We might define necking as being physical contact between the two sexes that expresses itself in hugging and kissing, cuddling, fondling, wandering hands, etc. Usually, it takes place in parked automobiles; they may be parked out by the side of the road. They may be parked in some secluded spot, or they may be parked at a drive-in theater. The geographical location does not matter; it is what takes place inside that I am talking about. Someone says, "Yes, but I know where to stop," I am not going to argue with you. You tell me that you know where to stop, I am just going to give you credit for having that much sense—that you *know* where to stop. But, now, let me ask you a question. When you get there, *will you want to stop?* If so, then you are the only person that God ever made that way. You are really unique. You know that necking is a chain reaction. It starts out in holding hands, kissing, hugging, cuddling, fondling, entwining of limbs and ends in sex betrayal. There is nothing wrong with that inside of marriage, but there is plenty wrong with it outside. You have no right to excite desires and passions which you have no God-given right to fulfill and to satisfy.

B. Let us notice what a few men have written on this subject. This is a little booklet called "Parking and Petting" and on page 5 you will find this: "Doctors will confirm the fact that absolutely nothing is more capable of arousing passion in a young man to the point where he may desire completion of the marriage act than petting." And the reason is simple. Petting *is* the beginning of the marriage act. You know the Bible mentions petting. It talks about the things I have described and it talks about them inside of marriage. For example, in Genesis 26:8, the King James Version says that Abimelech looked out and he saw Isaac "sporting" with Rebekah his wife. The Berkeley version says he saw Isaac "caressing" Rebekah his wife. The Revised Standard Version says that he saw Isaac "fondling" Rebekah his wife. This is not being condemned. They are married—they are husband and wife. It is part of the marriage act.

C. Let me give you this further definition of petting. Petting is used to prepare a wife to receive her husband. That is the purpose of it. That is the God-given reason for it, and unless you are married to each other you have no business engaging in it.

On page 11 of another tract, "Come Ye Out From Among Them," we find this: "That is why petting is dangerous, because it gets both parties to the point where they want to go further. Anyone who doesn't want to go the limit, therefore, has no business petting." "How to be Young and Enjoy It," page 23, states: "It is dangerous to trifle with the sex act, not only the complete one but any actions connected with it. When I say it is dangerous, I am not merely expressing my personal opinion. The statement is made because of the hundreds of tormented, unhappy, miserable people who have come to me with complicated emotional problems which have had their start in a sex sin of one degree or another."

D. I know that some of you are so far gone that it does not make any difference what God's word says about it, or what the preacher says, or what your mother and father say, you are going to go ahead and you are going to take your chances. Because you know, you have experimented, and you think you know, that you have self-control. However, there are those of you who want to know how to break this frustrating habit. So, I will give you three pieces of advice.

First of all, to *boys and girls.* If you really want to keep your bodies pure, "be not a partaker in other men's sins, keep thyself pure" (ITimothy 5:22), then stay out of parked cars. Stay in the light; stay away from the wrong crowds. Boys, don't do anything to your date which you would not want someone doing to your sister. Do unto her as you would have them do unto you. If you would not want someone to treat your own sister this way, then do not treat someone else's sister this way. Girls, you are so physically and biologically made that you have greater control over these emotions than the boys do. For that reason, to a great degree, you hold the safety and the goodness of your date in your hands. You set the standard, and he will live up to it. Suggest some alternative, with a smile — be kind. Stay out of these compromising situations.

CONCLUSION

A. Now, I realize that I have spoken quite frankly to you tonight. Young people, do you know why? Because you are young and because you have a treasure of infinite value in your youth. You have your life before you. You are at a time in life when it is easier to make decisions and stick by them than any other time. I know you think it is difficult, but you just wait until you get older. You are at a time in your life when it is easier to set the pattern for all your habits for the rest of your life. I do not want to see you get hurt. Do not engage in physical activities that will cause you to *think* you are in love when you are not. Then you get married and it is not long until you find that it was *lust* and not *love.* You are mismated and the only attraction was physical. My how difficult it is to get along with someone without the affinity of spirit and mind that you have to have to live richly in this close, intimate relationship. It becomes miserable and unbearable and finally you separate. You have not a God-given reason to remarry and you know that if you do you will lose your soul in hell. I hate to stand up here right now and look out into the faces of some of you who have already made this mistake—you married because of passion which you thought was love. The marriage did not last. You are young, handsome, pretty, you are warm blooded, you are very much alive and you know you are going to have to walk alone until death. I am being selfish in preaching this sermon. I do not want you to come to my office to get me to try to unravel the problem for you. I do not want you to come to my office and me have to tell you that you are going to have to live a chaste, single life all the days of your existence.

DO NOT PROSTITUTE YOUR LIFE

B. Do you know what the word "prostitute" means? It means to take something that was intended for one thing and not use it for that, but to use it for something for which it was not intended. That is what this word means. This microphone was intended to be used to pick up the sound waves of my voice and carry them to the amplifier and that is exactly what it is being used for. But if I took it off the stand and used it for a hammer, I would be prostituting the use of this microphone. Girls, I want you to know that God gave you your sex and your body for a holy purpose. Any time that you use it outside of wedlock to satisfy and to gratify the passions of your date, then you are a prostitute. I do not care whether you get any pay for it or not, you are a prostitute. You are prostituting the very body that God gave you. Am I your enemy because I tell you the truth? There is nothing so tragic in the world than to find young people who mistake lust for love, and then wise up too late. Isn't it strange that the world, the unconverted people, set a higher moral standard for us than we dare set for ourselves. Here is a young man or young lady who claims to be Christian and somebody in the world says, "Well, she may be a Christian, but I will tell you right now, she is really a hot date." They know there is something wrong. "He may be a Christian, but I tell you right now, he smokes a pack and a half of cigarettes a day." "He may claim to be a Christian, but he can drink more beer than anyone." Thus, the unconverted people of the world set a higher moral standard than we dare set for ourselves. Gal. 5 says, "The works of the flesh which are manifest are these; adultery, fornication, lasciviousness, uncleanness." Then verse 21 says, "I tell you again, as I have told you before, that they that do such things cannot inherit the kingdom of heaven." You have no right to stir up desires within your body that you have no right to fulfill. Americans are spending thousands and thousands of dollars each week on psychiatrists and psychologists to help them get rid of guilt complexes. There is just one place you can get rid of that guilt complex, and that is at the foot of the cross of Christ. It matters not how gravely you have sinned. It matters not how many times you may have sinned, there is pardon for you in the blood of Christ. Jesus said, "He that cometh to me, I will in no wise cast out." He will not reject you regardless of how bad, how vile you may have been, and the blood of Christ cleanseth us from all sins. Psalms 119:9 asks the question, "How shall the young man cleanse his way?" Then it answers, "By taking heed to the word."

STUDY QUESTIONS
GOD SPEAKS TO YOUTH

1. What is your attitude toward immorality of our nation?
2. What has God told us to do with regard to immorality?
3. Why has God said to "flee" certain things?
4. Did Joseph conduct himself properly in Potiphar's house?
5. What does "passion" mean?
6. What is "lasciviousness"?
7. Is the girl who dresses in immodest apparel as guilty of sin as the man who lusts after her?
8. Can a Christian say, "This is my life and I will do with it as I please"?
9. Why do boys start smoking?
10. Does filthy speech show a filthy heart?

AN OLD TESTAMENT DELINQUENT
(Judges 13, 14, and 15)

INTRODUCTION:
- A.   An Old Testament delinquent.
- B.   Delinquents in our time.

I. SAMSON
- A.   A personal description
- B.   Some of his exploits

II. DOES GOD ACT THROUGH MEN TODAY?
- A.   He did in Samson's day
- B.   He does do so today

III. SAMSON'S DELINQUENCY
- A.   Define delinquency
- B.   Samson had a sex problem
- C.   Samson had a parent problem
- D.   Samson had an ego problem
- E.   Young people have the same problems today

CONCLUSION:
- A.   Samson's repentance
- B.   Samson's death
- C.   The danger in delay

AN OLD TESTAMENT DELINQUENT
INTRODUCTION

There are several delinquents in the Old Testament, but the Old Testament Delinquent that I want to talk to you about is a boy named Samson. He had many things in common with all delinquents and with all young people today.

It has been my lot in the last few years to visit in several of the prisons in our land. As I have visited in these prisons, I have observed the inmates and have seen clean-cut, intelligent-looking young men going about their tasks. I have very often wondered just what went wrong in their lives. Then I pick up the Old Testament and I read about a clean-cut, intelligent, personable young man named Samson, and I wonder the same thing about him. Just what went wrong in his life? Human nature does not change. Since Samson had the same problems that boys and girls have today; we can analyze his life, character, and delinquency, then we'll have a lesson worthy of our consideration.

I.

Samson had many things in common with the youth today. One thing was that he was born in very troublesome times. He was born during a crisis in history. He, as you, was born in the time when there was great political, social and moral upheaval, and when old values were being scoffed at and discarded, and new moralities were suggested for men and women. He had a lot of characteristics, a lot of attributes, that make men love him and appreciate him. Let's get better acquainted with him. I always thrill at the opportunity to turn again and read Judges 13, 14, 15, and 16, about this cherished young man of Israel.

A. First of all, he was born to a rather common, ordinary family of godly parents. His father was named Manoah, and he was from the tribe of Dan. There was nothing unusual about this. They named him Samson, which in the Hebrew meant "sunshine" or "sunny". This young man was a fellow who was full of amusing pranks. He loved a good joke. He had a keen sense of humor. He was filled with cheer all of the time, everywhere that you saw him. He had a ringing laugh that would just drive the blues away. It's no wonder that Solomon said in Proverbs 15 that a merry heart doeth good like a medicine. And Samson truly had a merry heart. Now I don't care what other faults a person may have, if he radiates cheerfulness wherever he goes, he'll never be lacking for friends. Samson radiated cheerfulness wherever he went, and he always had a great group of friends gathered around him. Not only that, but he was a man of great physical courage. Now physical courage is not the highest type of courage, but it's the one that we admire the most. It's a courage that we have in kinship with a bulldog. I used to raise registered bulldogs, and they'd just as soon that you would sic them on a rhinoceros as any cat; it didn't matter, because they knew no fear at all. This man never had a tremor of fear. Never is it mentioned that he quaked before the enemy. Never is it mentioned that at any time goose flesh crawled over him when he was faced with an adversary. He had fine physical courage, and I imagine that the young boys idolized him. And I rather imagine that the boys, instead of playing cowboys and Indians or cops and robbers, probably played Samson and the Philistines.

B. He has another thing in his favor in that he was a great athlete. This is something else that compels us to admire him. I rather imagine that back in that half-savage age in which he lived that the admiration they had for him was almost worship. But we live in a civilized age, don't we? We claim that when we measure a man we don't measure his muscle, but rather we measure his head and measure his heart. But still, I'm afraid, the athlete grips our hearts perhaps more than the scholar. I rather imagine that if a great statesman had been lecturing last evening, and over in another assembly had been a great athlete, that athlete would have had the greater crowd by far. Now in all honesty, I must say that we remember the scholar and the poet and the statesman and the benefactor of mankind much longer than we remember the athlete. But nevertheless, while he is in his prime, he grips our hearts. That's the way Samson was.

C. Now let's notice a few things about his exploits. I realize that these things are quite academic to many of you, but maybe you can thrill again as I tell you of some of the things that happened to this particular choice young man of Israel. First of all in Judges 14 we find Samson going out and doing what all young teenage boys do—he was girl-hunting. He wasn't cruising up and down the streets in a hot-red automobile, but he was cruising down the trail going down to Timnath. He met a young lion, and Judges says that the lion roared against him. In other words, we have a confrontation here. This choice young man of Israel and a young lion were face to face in the narrow path, and Samson probably said something like this: "Lion, get out of my way. I've got a date; I'm going to Timnath." And the young lion roared against him. "Now I don't want to have any trouble with you, but if it's trouble you're looking for, we'll have it. Now step aside." We are told that Samson had nothing in his hands when he gathered him up and he rent him asunder, as he would have rent a kid goat. Not even Tarzan could do that! No wonder so many people respected Samson. He went on down to visit with his girlfriend; and in the process of time he was going down the same trail going to the same city to see the same woman, and he noticed that the bees had built a hive in the carcass of that lion. Samson went over and dug out some of the honey, and he ate it as he journeyed to Timnath. This was among the Philistines. And so Samson, being a fellow who enjoyed a good joke and having a keen sense of humor, thought that he would expound a riddle to them. He suggested that out of the eater came forth meat, and out of the strong came forth sweetness. Now he said, "If you can figure out what I'm talking about by the time the feast is over, I will give you 30 sheets and 30 changes of garments. If you can't figure it out, then you will have to give me 30 sheets and 30 changes of garments." But they couldn't figure it out. So they went to his espoused, and they asked her (she being a Philistine sister to them) to ask her espoused husband just what he was talking about. And so she came to him and she asked him to tell her the answer, and he said "I haven't even told my own father, my own mother, why should I tell you?" And then she began to turn all of the wiles of womanhood upon him, and she said "Now Samson, you just don't love me, or you'd tell me". This didn't work, so she pouted a little. Then she began to cry. Then like most men, he finally gave up and said, "All right", and he told her the answer to the riddle. Just as soon as she had an opportunity, she told her fellowmen. So when the hour came for the feast to end, Samson said, "Have you figured out the answer to the riddle I gave you?" and they said, "Yes, we believe that we have. We've been studying on this and thinking about it, and we just can't conceive of any beast stronger than a lion, nor anything sweeter than honey, so you must have gotten honey out of a lion." And everytime I read Samson's reply, I have to chuckle. He said, "If you had not plowed with my heifer, you would not have figured out my riddle." He's angry about this, because he's been betrayed. But nevertheless, he has made a bargain, and he's going to stick by it. So he went over to the neighboring city of Ashkelon and he slayed 30 Philistines, took their clothing, brought it and gave it to these men to whom he had promised it.

He asked for his wife, but the father-in-law said, "I thought you hated her, and I have already given her to someone else." Samson said, "You Philistines won't get away with this." So he went out and caught 300 foxes, tied torches to their tails, and turned them loose in the grain fields, and they burned the grain fields of the Philistines. Samson feared nothing. But word of this great conflagration had gotten back to his own people before he got there. His brethren got together and said, "He's going to get us into trouble. The Philistines aren't going to take this sort of thing. They're liable to come for reprisals." And so when Samson came, his own brethren took him and bound him and gave him to the Philistines. But we are told that the Spirit of the Lord came upon Samson, told that the Spirit of the Lord came upon Samson, and that he broke the cords with which he was bound, he took the jawbone of an ass and he slayed a thousand of them. And after this he was thirsty, so he took that same implement and dug a well to get a drink.

D. Another exploit of his that is pretty well-known is that he went into Gaza, the stronghold of the Philistines on a date one evening. The Philistines recognized him. Now he didn't have any giant proportions like King Saul. He was a man of ordinary build and ordinary stature, but he was just super-human in his strength. And so as the Philistines had recognized him inside the city limits, they gave orders to lock all the gates. They called out all the able-bodied men and boys so they could kill him. Samson, about midnight, decided he would go home; and so he came to the gates of the city, found them locked, but that didn't bother him. He just pulled them up: gateposts, hinges, bar and all. He carried them away to a mountain top in Hebron. That left Gaza without any gates, unprotected, and the virtual laughing stock of all the people round about. They determined that they would kill him. Where did he get the super strength that he had? It was not a natural physical gift. Now in a sense it was. Any gift that you and I have, physical or mental, came from God. But this was a supernatural gift which God had given him. It didn't come from training, I know, because if so, then other men would train just as hard and become just as strong as Samson. It was a gift that God gave him because of his vow of consecration to God. That's where it came from. Even before Samson was born his mother and father said "We're going to give him to God." As Samson began to grow up and to reach the age of reason, he assumed these vows of his parents. Now I'll readily admit that his consecration was far from perfect, but nevertheless, it enabled God to pour His spirit upon him, and to use him in the mighty way that He did. Without his consecration, God could not have used him. God gives His gifts in the same manner today. If you and I will trust in God, give our lives to Him, He will give us of His power, of His strength, and He will make us to glorify Him.

We read in Acts 5:32, "We are witnesses of these things and so also in the Holy Spirit whom God hath given unto all them that obey Him." 'But brother McKnight, does He do that today?' Let's move up into the 20th century and see. We've heard about the story of the movement of the city-wide census in Pasadena, Texas, of the Shaw Street congregation. These brethren decided to commit themselves to the Lord. By their own admission they were scared, frightened, but they were trusting in the Lord. And they went out for a house-to-house canvass in the city. They were overwhelmed that they found over 1700 families say, "Yes, we'd like to study the Bible with someone. Would you come and teach us?" One of the elders said, "Brother McKnight, the thing that makes me feel so badly is that God was waiting to use us all the time. Look how long He'd been waiting. The field was ripe and we were afraid to go in ourselves, to consecrate ourselves to God's service." And he said, "The only reason that we didn't go is because we didn't have more consecration. The reason we did what we did is because that's all the consecration we had." This year is 60 days old. Thirty people have obeyed the gospel here at Highland. I wonder how many there would have been if we were all totally consecrated to the Lord. God cannot feed us if we won't come to His table. He cannot bless us if we won't live in His house. He cannot walk with us if we will not walk with Him. This is the way that God blesses people today.

III.

Now, let us notice the delinquency of this young man. We've noticed everything else about him. The thing that impressed me about him is that he had the same problems that you teenagers have today.

I like to define terms before I use them, so that we'll know what we're talking about. Delinquency means "a failure in duty". Adults can be delinquent just the same as children. "Juvenile" means a young person. So a juvenile delinquent is a young person who has failed in his duty. And an adult delinquent is a grown person who has failed in his duty. Samson had about as much promise as any man in the Old Testament, and yet he failed miserably. Let us analyze some of the problems that he had here.

A. First of all I would suggest to you that Samson had a sex problem. Yes he did! He was no different from the prodigal son in the New Testament. He, too, had a sex problem. And teenagers today are being stimulated sexually by every means that the modern mind of man can conceive of: by sensuous music that bombards our ears day and night; by the radio, television, movies, magazines, billboard advertising, and everything else on every hand. Young people, God gave you sex. There is nothing dirty about it. There is nothing to be ashamed of. There is nothing vile nor vulgar about it. It is given for a high and holy reason. But the misuse of sex is a terrible sin against your God, against your fellow man, and against yourselves. You cannot experiment in sex. You cannot misuse this God-given passion, your appetite for sex, without sinning against God, against your neighbor, and without sinning against yourself. Paul writes about that very thing, in I Thessalonians 4:3-8. I'd like to read out of Phillip's Translation so that I won't have to do any explaining about what is said. Listen as Paul tells you that when you commit sins of sex you sin against God. He says in verse 3, "You will remember the instructions that we gave you then in the name of the Lord Jesus. God's plan is to make you holy, and that entails first of all a clean cut with sexual immorality." This is the first step, Paul says, toward holiness, a clean cut with sexual immorality. "Every one of you should learn to control your body, keeping it pure, and treating it with respect, and never regarding it as an instrument of self-gratification as do the pagans who have no knowledge of God." "You cannot break this rule without in some way cheating your fellow man, and you must remember that God will punish those who offend in this manner." "And we have warned you how that we have seen this work out in our own experience in life. The calling of God is not to impurity, but to the most thorough purity. And anyone who makes light of this matter is not making light of man's ruling, but of God's commandments; and it is not for nothing that the Spirit God gives us is called the

Holy Spirit." God did not say, "Thou shalt not commit adultery," because He didn't want you to enjoy life. Jesus said, "I have come that you may have life, and that you may have it abundantly." That you may live life to the hilt, to the fullest! Our God is not a God who goes around with a stick in His hand, hitting people on the head to keep them from enjoying themselves. Then why did God give these restrictions and these restraints? Because God knows that the family, the home, is the basic unit of the society in which we live, and that if the sanctity of the marriage vows and the sacredness of the home is violated, then the very basic unity of our society will crumble. God knows that would be to our detriment, to our hurt, to our everlasting and eternal shame. God knows that if you misuse sex, it will harden your heart against Him, and that it will cause you to forsake Him quicker than any other sin. That's the reason He said it.

B. Samson not only had a sex sin, but he also had a parent problem. A teenager said the other day, "Parents are such a problem." And every normal teenager in the world can say a hearty "amen" to that. Yes, parents are. Samson had a problem with parents, the Prodigal had a problem with parents, and you have a problem with your parents. If you've already passed that age, you used to have a problem with your parents. Let us just look at it objectively and see what we can get out of this. First of all I would readily concede that some parents are a problem. I know a young man who is attempting to make a preacher of the Gospel. His father is a drunkard, and discourages him on every hand. That father is a real problem. I know another young man planning to make a preacher who is from a divorced, a divided, a broken home. Neither side of the home is godly; they are worldly; they laugh at him; they mock him; they make fun of him. Both parents are real problems.

A well known Gospel preacher said, "After I was born, my parents never lived together. When I was eleven years old, my mother was killed in an automobile accident, and I went to live with a 74 year old grandmother who had no business attempting to rear a young boy. You teenagers think that you have a problem with the parents that you have. You ought to try growing up in this old world as an orphan. Your parents love you more than they love life itself, and you ought to thank God for it." Yes, I realize there are parents who are real problems. Now let's move up to average parents. They are a real problem to teenagers. When daddy talks real goodly about honesty and about putting the right values on things in life, then the teenager sees him sit all evening in front of the television set sipping beer. They forget about his lecture, but remember what he does. And he talks so goodly about honesty being a great virtue and then the teenagers hear him tell white lies on the telephone. They forget his lecture, but they remember what he does. Parents, what kind of values are you instilling in the hearts of your teenage children? What things are important to you? Does the color television take precedence over everything else in the household? Is it the most important thing there? Do you give more time and attention to it than to anything else? Is buying a new car everytime the models change the most important thing in your life? If so, then you are rearing children who will know what was most important to you. Some day they'll say "Well, mom and dad thought that the cocktail party was more important than the church." "My mother and father spent more time planning where we'd spend a vacation than where we'd spend eternity, so the vacation must be the more important." "My daddy and mother paid more for the color television set than they gave to the Lord in a whole year." "My mother and father thought that buying a new car was more important than supporting a missionary to preach the gospel." These are the kind of values your teenagers are learning from you, parents.

Don't you think they can see through your hypocrisy? Do you think your teenage sons and daughters are a bunch of nincompoops? Don't you know they can see through that inconsistency? It is no wonder that they rebel against your kind of religion! I thank God that they do! You know there are many of our boys and girls today that are not buying the old hogwash that mother and daddy are attempting to poke down their throats about going to state universities and state colleges and making doctors and lawyers and things like this because they can make more money! We have teenagers today who know that there are things more important in life than making money. Thank God for them! And some of them know more than their own parents in that respect. Teenagers, don't you ever let your mothers and daddys pull you down from the high and holy purpose of life. Give yourself to something that will outlast life itself. And I suggest to you that if there is not anything more important than making money in life, commit suicide today! Some of you parents need to grow up. You need to start instilling some Christian principles in the hearts of these young people. That is where their problem lies.

Even good parents are a problem. We just got through talking about the average, normal parents. Now I'm talking about good parents, godly people. They are a problem, because you teenagers want to live your life like you want to live it, and you want to go where you want to go, and do what you want to do, without any restrictions, rules, regulations or restraints on you. That is what you want. And so it is necessary that even godly parents are a problem to you. Good parents know more than you know. I know you do not believe that, but your mothers and fathers are smarter than you are. They have learned a lot of things in lessons from hard knocks along life's road, they know where most of the slippery places are, most of the sharp curves are, and they don't want you to get hurt. That is the reason they say "no".

It is no wonder that in God's Word we are told "Children, obey your parents in the Lord, for this is right." It is no wonder that God, in His Holy Word says "Honor thy father and thy mother". Listen to this: a Chinese boy or girl would rather die than bring dishonour on their family. There has never been one case of juvenile delinquency among the millions of Chinese Americans who live in our metropolitan areas because the children had rather die than to bring dishonor on their parents.

Yes, good parents are a problem, aren't they? Proverbs 1:8 says, "Son, hear the instructions of thy father. Forsake not the law of thy mother."

Let us go back to Samson and a problem he had with his parents. Samson went down to Timnath and there he saw a girl, a daughter of the Philistines. And he came back home and told his mother and father that he had found the girl for him, "she's down in Timnath, a daughter of the Philistines. Get her for me, for she pleaseth me well." Samson said, "She's just what I want. Now go get her." He had godly parents; look at the problem they had on their hands. They had a little family squabble right here. His mother and father tried to reason with him: "Now Samson, look at the daughters of Israel all around you, some of them exceedingly fair. Why do you have to go out and get a daughter among the uncircumcised Philistines?" And Samson's bottom lip turned down! He sat there and pouted. And he began to tell them, "Well you just don't love me. If you did, you'd get what I want." You know what Samson is doing? He's doing the very thing that every normal teenager does. He's reaching out to see if his parents have built a barrier or a fence out there somewhere. Every normal teenager is going to go as far as his parents will let him. Now that's just all there is to it. And he's reaching out there to see if they have put up a fence. If they haven't, he's going to push them a little farther, and a little farther. That is just as normal as life itself.

A college official was telling about his 16-year-old son, who plays in a band. He came in and said, "Daddy, our little band just had an offer for a job to play at a dance. Is it alright with you if I go and play? I won't dance or anything, but I'd like to play in the band." Here's what his daddy said, "Now son, I'd just as soon you would go up to the bar and drink as to mix the drinks for someone else. I'd just as soon you were out there dancing, as playing in the band for someone else." Then the son said, "Daddy, what's wrong with it?" See, he is feeling for the fences. His daddy said, "Son, I'll tell you what's wrong with it. As long as you're sixteen years old, and you stay in my house, and you eat my groceries, you're not going to do it." He said, "you know, that boy understood that. I haven't had any more problems."

An elder of the church sat in my living room just a few days ago, and he said "Mid, the dean of the college here did something for me that I don't have the courage to do. He told my son 'You've got to take that car home.' I just didn't have the moral courage. I know he didn't need it. And I know it was hurting his grades, and the dean had to do something that I didn't have the courage to do." I don't care who the child is, they are going to reach out there for those fences. And when you say, now this is it; this is as far as you can go, they are going to push on it. And they are going to try to see if you really mean it. If we move the fence over a little, they are going to push a little harder, and a little harder, and a little harder. Now a parent who will not erect these fences is a mighty poor parent. And I'll say again to you parents, if you don't erect these barriers for your children, you don't love them! Suppose one of my boys comes up to me and says, "Daddy, give me $5.00. I want to buy some liquor." "Now, son, do you really think you ought to do this?" "Yes, Daddy, everybody else is doing it." Here we go with those arguments. If one of my boys asks me a question like that, I won't have to answer him with but one two-letter word. There won't be any argument, and he will know what I mean. Now he may learn to drink, but he's going to have to learn it from you.

A broken-hearted father sat in my living room this week, and he said, "Mid, I taught my teenage son to smoke. And I did a good job. He smokes one cigarette right after the other from the time he wakes up until the time he goes to bed. But I can't say anything to him, because I taught him."

C. Samson had a sex problem, he had a problem with parents. Parents are a problem. It's because we love you that we tell you 'no'. Oh, I know. We are human. We may not go about it in the right way. We may be harsh, or cruel, but it's because we love you. If we did not love you we would not say 'no'. We would let you go, and the sooner the better. But Samson had another problem, and that was a problem with his ego—his self-sufficiency. He was just like every other teenager. He was man enough to stand on his own two feet, go where he wanted to, do what he pleased, without having to say anything to anyone, he thought. He went on to Gaza, the stronghold of the Philistines, and had an affair with one of the Philistine women. It did not bother him nor scare him. He was a big, tough fellow. That is, until we find him grinding in the prison house with both of his eyes gouged out. I Corinthians 10:12: "Let him that thinketh he stand, take heed lest he fall." Proverbs 16:23: "He that ruleth his own spirit is better than he that taketh a city." Unless you learn to control yourself, you will never excel in any field. Unless you learn self-discipline, you will never succeed in any field. Some men cannot make good insurance salesmen because they do not have enough self-discipline to get themselves out of bed and calling on prospects. Some people cannot lose any weight because they do not have enough self-discipline to push back from the table. Some people cannot quit smoking because they do not have enough self-discipline to quit smoking. Others cannot quit drinking because they do not have enough self-discipline to quit. You cannot excel in any field until you learn how to control yourself. Proverbs 5:22: "Ye shall be holden of the cords of your own sin." Young people, you may be self-sufficient, you may be pretty smart, and you may have fooled your parents. You may have even fooled the law enforcement agency of our city, of our country, but you cannot fool God! You shall be holden of the cords of your own sins. The moment that we step aside from the pathway of righteousness, we begin to bind our souls in chains. None of us are smart enough to be exempt.

I am sure that had the preacher or the parents of the two University coeds told these girls, "Now you don't have any business going up into James Cross's apartment to bathe and to change clothes", they would have responded, "Why, we live in the 20th Century, and we enjoy greater freedoms than anyone else has ever had. We don't live under Queen Victoria any more. Those old Puritan ideas have been done away with. We live under the new morality. We're free. I can take care of myself." But they are both dead today. And James Cross is facing a lifetime in prison because of it. I don't know if he ever read Proverbs 5:22 or not, but he fulfilled it. He said those 19 days, from the day that he killed these two girls until he confessed, was a life of hell. He said, "I lived in turmoil". You will be held accountable! You can't escape it. You're going to pay for it. Everyone else will. It does not matter who they are.

I was counseling with a young lady who is another fulfillment of Proverbs 5:22. "Brother McKnight, I've got to have some help. I have slipped into the sex trap. I have been intimate with various and sundry ones. I knew all the time it was wrong, and I hated myself, but now I've met a fine Christian boy. He wants me to marry him. Brother McKnight, I am not fit to be his wife. I am not fit to be the mother of his children. I've thought about killing myself." You shall be holden with the cords of your own sins. I assured her, as she had repented, that in God's eyes, she is just as pure as any virgin in this city. But still, "you shall be holden with the cords of your own sins." Sin does not make you free, young people. It binds you! Listen to Job 4:8: "Those that plow wickedness and sow iniquity shall reap the same thing." Numbers 32:23, God said, "Be sure your sins will find you out." Galatians 6:7, paraphrasing for the sake of clarity, "Be not deceived. You cannot make a mockery of God. Whatsoever a man soweth, that shall he also reap. If you sow to the flesh, you shall of the flesh reap corruption, and if you sow to the spirit, you shall of the spirit reap everlasting life." John 8:34: "Whosoever commiteth sin is a bondservant of sin." Two verses later, John 8:26: "If the Son shall make you free, then shall you be free indeed."

CONCLUSION

Let us go back to Samson as we close this lesson. Samson has paid for his sin. He has been blinded in the prison house. The Philistines are having a big religious holiday. They are celebrating and honoring Dagon, their god. They said, "Bring Samson out of the prison house, and let him make sport for us, let him entertain us." All of the high officials of the Philistine government were there. All of the lords and ladies of the Philistines were gathered in this great temple of Dagon. They thought that Dagon was greater than Samson's God, because "our god has delivered Samson into our hands." Samson is leaning against two tremendous columns that support the ceiling.

This is about a half-open type theater, and there are hundreds of people upon the roof of the building watching. The building is filled. Listen to Samson, now, as he prays his last prayer: "Oh, God, remember me. I pray thee, Oh, God, give me back my strength just this once." Look at the power in a sincere, fervent prayer. He shoved the columns apart and the roof fell in, and he killed more Philistines in his death than he ever did in his life. I take the text of this prayer to suggest that Samson has repented. God is going to carry out his program of work whether you and I cooperate or not. If we go against Him, it is to our own detriment.

The ship Stanley Whitney was sailing from Ireland a few years ago with immigrants bound for America got in a gale that drove it aground on the southern coast of Ireland. For just a few moments, the bow of the ship perched upon the cliff of the bank. The captain saw that the situation was perilous, even hopeless, and he warned everyone to go ashore. Quite a few people seized the opportunity and went onto the bow of the ship and onto the shore. But a few hesitated. And in a few minutes the ship slipped, and went down in the turbulent waters of the sea, and all who hesitated were lost.

Is there a man, woman, boy or girl today who will pray with all the fervor of your heart, "Oh, God, give me the strength just this once to do what I know I ought to do?"

This writer is indebted to Clovis G. Chappell for permission to use some of the thoughts and excerpts found in this lesson which are from his book, *Sermons on Old and New Testament Characters.*

STUDY QUESTIONS
AN OLD TESTAMENT DELINQUENT

1. What is the meaning of Samson's name?
2. What primary thing caused people to admire him?
3. Whom did his parents desire him to marry?
4. Does God work through man today?
5. Define delinquency.
6. Can adults be delinquent?
7. Are God's commandments to keep us from having a good time? Explain.
8. Who has the greatest influence in molding the lives of our children?
9. Why did Samson go wrong?
10. Does the parent who refuses to "build fences" really love his children?

GOD'S WILL CONCERNING THE AGED
(Titus 2:1-5)

INTRODUCTION:
   A. Not many will admit being aged
   B. Some elderly people are happy and cheerful while others are sullen and sour
   C. Psalms 90:10
   D. Vain attempts to stay young
   E. Philippians 1:21

I. VALUABLE WORK FOR ELDERLY TO DO:
   A. Be an example in purity and in holiness
      1. Physical activities are restricted
      2. Example and encouragement to younger people
   B. Titus 2:1-5

II. OTHER WORK FOR ELDERLY:
   A. Well fitted for counselship and advice
      1. Job 12:12
      2. Good judgment comes through experience
   B. "Old men for counsel, young men for action"
      1. I Kings 12
      2. Folly of seeking advice from inexperienced
      3. Why God placed elders over the church

III. OUR RESPONSIBILITY TO OUR OWN AGED:
   A. Young people owe honor to the aged
      1. Ephesians 6:1
      2. I Timothy 5:8
      3. I Timothy 5:4
   B. Young people owe respect to the aged
      1. Leviticus 19:32
      2. Proverbs 23:22
      3. Proverbs 16:31

IV. EXHORTATION TO FAITHFULNESS:
    A.   Aged should remain faithful
    B.   Body will decay but soul will live forever

CONCLUSION:
    A.   Revelation 2:10
    B.   Revelation 14:13

GOD'S WILL CONCERNING THE AGED
(Titus 2:1-5)
INTRODUCTION

A. I realize the subject we have for this morning is one which is not preached very much. Nevertheless, the scriptures are not silent concerning God's will for the aged. Perhaps one reason that the lesson is not preached more often is because you can rarely find a person who will admit being in this classification. However, if we live long enough we will be aged some day. We need to begin now to prepare to grow old gracefully.

B. Have you ever noticed old people who are happy, cheerful, and still a blessing to those with whom they come in contact and are still useful to society, to the church, and to the home? On the other hand, we find those who have soured on life; life's experiences have embittered them, they are pessimistic and they make life miserable for themselves and for others all around about them. The difference is in our attitude toward old age. God teaches us concerning the attitude which we should have. I can think of one couple in particular, in their 80's, who love each other so much, who are so happy and cheerful that they bring a ray of sunshine wherever they go. They are a source of inspiration and encouragement to many of us who are younger. Many of us have decided to pattern our lives after theirs. So, we want to talk to you a little while about growing old. Growing old is not so bad when you consider there is just one alternative. Let's hope that we all grow old, and let us grow old gracefully in the service of the Master.

C. When we talk about growing old, we should use the scriptural definition of it; Psalms 90:10 tells us our "days are threescore and ten and if by reason of strength they should be fourscore, soon they are cut off and we fly away." So the average span of mankind is about 70 and this is just about the life expectancy of a child being born in the U.S.A. today. There are those, of course, who exceed this time which is alloted them and there are those who fall short of it. I think there should be no fear of old age on the part of anyone. To me, it is utterly ridiculous for someone to be ashamed of their age and to keep it like a closely guarded secret. American people are those, above all other people in the world, who fear old age.

D. Newspapers, magazines, television and radio commercials are always telling us about something that will keep us looking young, acting young and being young. Yet, there is not enough pancake make-up in the world to take one second off of your age. There is not enough health food in the world to take one year, one week, one day or one hour off of our ages. I think the most ridiculous thing which I see in the modern society is a grandmother trying to look and act like a young lady of 18 or 20. Age is just as natural as nature itself and these bodies were not meant to last forever. They were meant to house our souls temporarily until the Master shall call us home. In Job 5:26, He says, "Thou shalt come to thy grave in full age like a shock of wheat in its season." It is a natural thing, and a very beautiful thing to see someone who has lived a rich, full and useful life in the Master's kingdom to come down to the end of life and to go to his grave at peace with God and at peace with his fellowman.

E In Philippians 1:21, Paul has this to say, "For me to live is Christ, but for me to die is gain." This is the way he could look out upon life, and upon the life eternal. When you have given yourself to the service of the Master and come down to the harvest time of life, you can look back upon a duty well done, and you can look forward to a crown nearly won. This is the way that old age ought to be.

I.

Now there is some valuable work for old people to do which the Master has mentioned. One of them mentioned in the scripture reading for this morning –set an example in purity and holiness. Those who have reached the age in which they are not too useful as far as doing manual labor; their energies have been sapped by many years of living, can be such a great encouragement to those of us who are younger.We can look to you and see there a true child of God. Certainly, there is no excuse regardless of the age which you may be, to ever cease to set a good example in purity and in holiness.

B. In the scripture text which was read a moment ago, Paul said to Titus: "Speak the things which become sound doctrine." Some of the things he said were; "Tell the aged men that they are to be sober (serious minded), grave and temperate; sound in the faith, sound in love and sound in patience. Let the aged women likewise, be in behavior as becometh Godliness; not false accusers (not gossipers or slanderers), teachers of good things that they may teach the younger women to be sober, chaste, discreet, to love their husbands and to love their own children." Let's read it out of Phillip's translation if you will. It puts it in a language we can understand. Paul writes to Titus and he said, "Now you must tell them the sort of character which should spring from sound teaching. The old men should be temperate, serious, wise—spiritually healthy through their faith and love and patience. Similarly the old women should be reverent in their behavior, should not make unfounded complaints and should not be overfond of wine. They should be examples of the good life, so that the younger women may learn to love their husbands and their children, to be sensible and chaste, home lovers, kindhearted and willing to adapt themselves to their husbands—a good advertisement for the Christian faith." God expects those who are older in years to set the proper example for those who are younger. It is so easy today to pattern your life after one who you have walked with, to pattern your speech after one who you have heard, but it is so difficult when one says one thing and then does another. So, God expects those who are older to set the proper example for us.

II.

A. In regard to the work of the old people, counselship and advice come from them and they are well fitted for it. I know they are well fitted because God says that they are. Many times, we who are younger cheat ourselves out of a good legacy in this life by not listening to the words of counselship and advice that come from those who have lived in very trying experiences and perhaps through all of the experiences of life that you and I shall have. We read in Job 12:12, "With the ancient is wisdom, and in length of days understanding." With those who have reached a ripe old age there is wisdom and it can only be learned one way and that is through experience. That is the only way you can get it. There are not enough books in the world to make us wise in the ways of life and in human relationships without living it. Good judgment comes through experience. Older people have had far more experiences than we who are younger. Good judgment comes from experience and experience comes from bad judgment. There are some lessons in life we just have to learn the hard way, it seems. Who is there among us who could say, "I have never made a mistake, I have never exercised any bad judgment." But bad judgment brings experiences and we can base our future actions on those experiences and good judgment comes from experience.

B. This is an old adage, "Old men for counsel and young men for action." This is the way God arranged it. This is the reason that one of the qualifications for elders is that they not be novices, but men of experience. The elder is to be of the older group of men because of his experiences. We make many mistakes many times when we go to the counselship of young men. I think of a young man back in I Kings 12 who made that mistake. Rehoboam has inherited the kingdom from his father, Solomon. Jeroboam comes with a delegation of the people and says, "Rehoboam, we want to know something. You have a decision to make. Are you going to lower the taxes or not?" Rehoboam said, "Give me three days to think it over, and then come back." Rehoboam went first to the older men, the men who had served as judges under his father and these older men gave him counselship and advice. They said, "Rehoboam, your father has built a mighty kingdom. The children of Israel have borne a tremendous load in establishing this kingdom and building it up to the magnificence that it has. Why don't you show them how much you love and appreciate them by lowering their taxes and easing their burdens." That was the counselship and advice of the old men. But Rehoboam then went to his cohorts, the men of about his age and said, "What would you do if you were the king?" Listen to the counselship that they gave. They said, "Why don't you build on the foundation that your father has lain? Why don't you make a bigger kingdom than he ever thought about?" Whose advice are you going to follow, Rehoboam? Experience or inexperience? It is lamentable, indeed, that he decided to follow the counselship of the younger men. When Jeroboam came back and asked for a decision, Rehoboam said, "I will tell you what my decision is. Whereas my father chastised you with whips, I will chastise you with scorpions. You see my little finger," he boasted, "my little finger is going to be bigger than my father's thigh." In other words, you think Solomon was a great man, but you haven't seen anything yet, and we know the tragic consequences of the divided kingdom. He hadn't followed the advice based upon experience in life from the old men. Both are essential to getting the work done, and God so arranged it that way. Many old people have lost their vitality. Those who have reached that age can give good counselship and and advice, but many times they do not have the physical health and stamina to carry it out. So look to the old for counsel and look to the young for action. This is the reason that the God of heaven in His infinite wisdom has placed the elders as the overseers of the church and has placed the deacons and those who are younger in the special charge of carrying out the physical, menial tasks of the operation of the congregation.

I can remember an elder who was a wonderful old man. He never had much formal education. His grammar wasn't exactly the best, but he knew the Book and he knew the book of life. My own father died when I was 20 years old. Many times I went to Brother G. A. Davis with problems, especially concerning the kingdom. He was always happy, and he was always cheerful. He was always very optimistic. He always could give some good, solid advice. When he died, I made a statement in front of some other men about how I was going to miss him. Every young man in that group said the same thing. All of us had been going to him with our problems for counselship and advice. Older people, those of you who are approaching old age, equip your lives so you can serve in this capacity. How we need someone who we can turn to. How we need someone, who in life's experiences, has been well educated in the problems of human relations and in carrying out the Master's work.

When I go back to visit one city, one of the first houses I call on is of a man 86 years old. He is a retired gospel preacher who has been invaluable in assisting me to do the work that I attempt to do for the Master. How I look forward to visiting with him. He is getting old in years, his eyesight is dimmed, he is a diabetic, but he never complains. He never whimpers and whines. He is always looking on the bright side of life and he has always got a lot of counselship and advice that would be good for anyone to follow. This is what God intended for the aged.

III.

A. Now with regard to the aged in the home, I would like to say a few words, because the God of Heaven has left instruction in this regard.

Young people owe a lot to the aged in the Home. One thing that we owe is honor. "Honor thy father and thy mother." We have talked about that in lessons previously. I will say no more about it, but I want to use a passage of scripture in its rightful way, in its very fundamental sense. I Timothy 5:8 is talking to the younger people and it is talking about taking care of the older people physically and financially. It says, "If any provide not for his own (aged) he hath denied the faith and he is worse than an infidel." Now I think the principle works both ways. If a man doesn't provide for his own children, he has denied the faith. But if you will take the context in which I Timothy 5:8 was written, it is talking about children's responsibility to the aged and it said, "if any man provide not for his own, he hath denied the faith and he is worse than an infidel." This is the true context and the true meaning under which those words were written. We have a responsibility to those who are older.

Then in I Timothy 5:4, he said, "But if any widow have children or nephews, let the children first learn to show piety at home and to requite their parents." This is pretty plain, isn't it? If any widow have children or grandchildren, is what the true translation means, let them learn to show piety at home and let them provide the things which are necessary to sustain life. Then it continues in the same vein in the 16th verse of the fifth chapter and says, "If any man or woman that believeth hath widows, let them relieve them. Let the church be not charged, that the church might take care of those who are widows indeed." God in his plan for the aged has intended that when their earning ability is curtailed those who are younger, those who have what they have because of the sacrifice of the older, will take care of them and see that they are provided for. Not only honor, but personal respect and courtesy is due them.

Many times young people look upon older people in the home as a terrible burden. This is no way for an old person, one who has given you life, given you health, has cared for you in your youth, to have to make an exit from this life, is it?

B. Let's notice what God has said in regard to our respect for these older people. In Leviticus 19:32, "Thou shalt rise up before the hoary head (the old head). Thou shalt honour the face of the old man." Courtesy and respect is demanded by God. Again in Proverbs 23:22, "Hearken unto thy father that did begat thee and despise not thy mother when she is old." It sounds strange that these admonitions should have to be given to God's children, but sometimes it is essential to remind them. There is honor in the hoary head because Solomon said so in Proverbs 16:31. He said, ". . . .the hoary head is a crown of glory, if it be found in the way of righteousness." *If* it be found in the way of righteousness. That is the key to it. When you come down to the sunset of life, in order not to look back upon a life misspent and a life misused, you are going to have to live it right, right now. I sat yesterday in my office and read a letter from a prisoner, written from the County jail, waiting to be transferred to prison for 15 years. He was writing the story of his life. Yes, after he gets out, he can dedicate himself to the service of the Master, but there is always going to be that blot and that blight in his memory. There is only one way to keep that from plaguing you in the sunset of your life and that is to live a life now so you won't have those regrets to look back upon, such as that man does have.

IV.

A. The aged should remain faithful. A preacher stopped in one time to visit an elderly lady. She was nearly 100 years old. She was a saint of God and she lived alone. The preacher suggested to her, "Don't you get lonely out here?" And she said, "No, because God and Christ have been with me for many years." "When did you obey the gospel?" She said, "At the age of 16." She had walked with her Master for some 80 years. As the preacher started to leave, she said, "I have been scribbling some lines of poetry. I would like for you to take them and read them; I don't know how good they are, but they express the sentiment of my heart." I have a copy of them here before me. Listen to this woman nearly 100 years old, as she says:

"This old shell in which I dwell
Is growing old, I know full well,
But I am not the shell.
What if my hair is turning gray,
Gray hair is honorable, they say.
What if my sight is growing dim,
I still can see to follow Him.
What should I care if times old plow
Has left deep furrows on my brow.
Another house, not made with hands,
Awaits me in the Glory Land.
What tho my tongue refuse to talk,
What tho I falter in my walk,
I still can tread the narrow way,
I still can sing, and watch and pray.
My hearing may not be as keen
As in times past it may have been
But I still can hear the Savior say
In whispers soft, "This is the Way."
This outward man, do what I can,

To lengthen out his life's short span,
Shall perish and return to dust,
As everything in nature must.
The inward man, the scriptures say,
Is growing stronger every day.
Then how can I be growing old
When safe within the Master's fold?
Ere long this soul shall fly away
And leave this tenement of clay.
This robe of flesh I'll drop and rise
To seize the "everlasting prize."
I'll meet you on the streets of gold
And prove that I'm not growing old!

B. The body will decay and go back to the dust of the earth from whence it came, but the soul shall live forever. There is no need of your soul decaying away. There is no need of your soul rotting in your body. Give yourself unto the Master. Paul came down to the close of his life, an old man and his body racked with pain and marked with wounds which he had received. You remember his words, He said, "For I am now ready to be offered. The time of my departure is at hand, but I have fought a good fight. I have kept the faith. I have finished the course and henceforth there is laid up for me a crown of righteousness and not for me only but for all those that love his appearing." Death held no fears for him. He had no regrets in life. Yes, he had made mistakes, but he knew he had done the best he could. Can you say this today? Are you doing the best you can?

CONCLUSION

For young and old alike, Revelation 2:10 says, "Be thou faithful unto death, and you shall receive the crown of life." Revelation 14:13, "Blessed are the dead that die in the Lord, they shall rest from their labors and their works do follow them." If you are not living for Him, the only way in the world that you can grow old gracefully and let those years be the years of harvest and of honor, is to give yourself to Him completely and wholeheartedly by obeying the gospel or by rededicating your life if you need to.

STUDY QUESTIONS
GOD'S WILL CONCERNING THE AGED

1. What is the average life span of man?
2. Discuss Titus 2:2-5.
3. Why are older people especially equipped to give good advice?
4. Analyze the contention that often exists between youth and old age.
5. Discuss the adage, "Old men for counsel and young men for action."
6. Do you see the need for both elders and deacons in a church?
7. Who gave Rehoboam bad advice?
8. What do the younger people "owe" the older people in the home?
9. The body must grow old. Is there any need for the spirit to grow old?
10. Are you preparing now for a happy and cheerful old age?